The Booby Blog

A Cancer Chronicle

Hollis Walker

OSIRIS
HOUSE
santa fe

Published by:
Osiris House LLC
P.O. Box 32553
Santa Fe, New Mexico 87594
www.osirishouse.com

Printed in the United States of America
First Edition: October 2014

Excerpt from "Kindness" from *Words Under the Words: Selected Poems*
by Naomi Shihab Nye, © 1995. Reprinted with permission of Far
Corner Books, Portland, Oregon

Cover art: "Call Upon My Blessed Passion #2" by Alexandra Eldridge
Author photo: Kitty Leaken
Front cover design: Alex Hanna/Invisible City Designs
Book design: Bad Dog Design/Santa Fe

Library of Congress Control Number: 2014912544
ISBN: 978-0-9905707-07

10 9 8 7 6 5 4 3 2 1

for Karen

Introduction

On the morning of October 23, 2012, I awoke with a voice in my head. Though I was still floating in that fuzzy netherworld between dream and reality, The Voice was clear: "You have a lump in your left breast." Somehow I knew it was cancer, and I knew that somehow it represented years of accumulated grief. Within the few weeks it took to get a definitive diagnosis, I also came to know that in dealing with this cancer, I would be propelled further along the spiritual path on which I had embarked almost five years before. I knew instinctively that this fearsome challenge would prove to be part of what I needed to learn in life and that what I learned from it someday might be of use to others.

Thus began my yearlong journey through cancer. Many numinous events occurred along the way that reinforced my sense that this experience was part of my spiritual destiny. Everything—good *and* bad—seemed fated.

This book has felt the same way. Almost as soon as I was diagnosed, I realized I would have difficulty keeping in touch with my circle of family members and friends as things developed. How would I ever remember what I had told which person? I decided a blog was in order, and when I sat down to write the first one, it seemed obvious to call it the Booby Blog and the recipients my Bosom Buddies. I vowed to myself to keep it honest and recognized from the beginning that for me—a lifelong journalist and personal journal keeper—writing the blog would really serve me more than those to whom it was sent. Or so I thought.

The list quickly grew from 10 people to include many others, as word spread among friends that I had cancer. People who received it wrote back to me, sometimes passionately, of experiences they and their loved ones had had that were similar to mine. Some friends passed it along to other people they knew who had breast cancer or other illnesses. The interaction fed my soul and consistently lifted my spirits.

Yet I didn't feel I could share all of my experience with others. I didn't want to sound like a whiner or a crybaby. Every day I met people struggling with medical problems much more serious than mine; how could I complain? But suffering is relative. I can walk with aplomb through a life challenge that would slay you, and vice versa. Awareness of this paradox didn't relieve me of its inherent tension. So in addition to my ordinary daily journaling, a sort of knee-jerk mental discharge process I've practiced since my teens, I started a separate journal that I called my Cancer Chronicle. In it I felt freer to bitch and moan about the insensitivity of health caregivers and the failings of Western medicine and to go rounds with the thornier existential questions about having a life-threatening disease.

As my treatment was coming to an end, several close friends in the Bay Area were diagnosed with breast cancer, and I was introduced to others who had breast cancer in my hometown of Santa Fe. I started wishing I had the Booby Blog in some format in which I could share it. Yet when I talked with those friends, it was those "thornier" issues that I'd tackled in the Cancer Chronicle that arose most quickly in our conversations. I could see that we were all struggling with the same questions, the same concrete and intangible issues. I began to imagine that I could collect both the Booby Blogs and my Cancer Chronicle entries into one readable form.

Here is the book I envisioned. I have edited little in the blogs or the journal entries, but I have changed names to protect the privacy of those who might not wish to be named. I have also deleted some journal entries in cases where they were redundant with the blogs.

I am not foolish enough to imagine that I have answers for anyone but me when it comes to making choices about how to deal with breast cancer. I'm not in the business of giving medical advice. What I hope to impart to others who have cancer or similar life-threatening diseases is that *we can be the authors of our own healing.* In fact, we must be.

If you have cancer or another serious illness, listen up: No one else—no doctor, no family member, no friend, no clergy member, no one but you—is going through this. You are the star of this drama, and as the leading lady (or man), while you are not entirely in control of the show, you certainly should get to call a lot of the shots. Practitioners and treatments of all kinds may help, but ultimately you are responsible for yourself and your own healing. And by healing I don't necessarily mean physical cure. The disease process may continue, or may disappear only to reappear, but we can still find healing in our emotional, spiritual and relational lives. The pursuit of healing is an end in itself.

May you find in this little book inspiration to help you on your own path with illness. May you discover that you no longer need to place the authority for your healing in the hands of others. May you learn to trust your own inner wisdom as you make decisions about your care. May you find the strength to share your journey with others who are in need of support. May you be healed.

Booby Blog #1

December 1

Dear Friends and Family:

I wanted to let you all know about an issue I'm having with my health, but I wanted to make it easy on myself, hence you are getting a group email. I've decided to call you my "Bosom Buddies."

Yesterday I learned that the lump I discovered in my breast in late October is cancerous. I went to the Santa Fe radiology practice where I had gone in 2008. At that time, a suspicious area was discovered, and I had a needle biopsy that showed it was benign. This latest experience had the sense of déjà vu, only this time the needle biopsy showed the lump to be malignant.

The next step is getting approved for the financial assistance I need, since I don't have health insurance. Then I will have an MRI, through which the docs will get a more specific picture of the booby's troubled tissue. Then they'll make recommendations. One likely outcome is a lumpectomy. Beyond that, my "breast imaging navigator," a wonderful RN at the radiologist's office, says not to project. I think that's wise.

I expected this outcome for a lot of reasons, so I am not really shocked or particularly scared. I figure this is just another part of my spiritual journey. I've decided I will create a new altar honoring this part of my journey, so if you'd like to, please send me an image (a postcard, photo or magazine picture will suffice) or a poem or whatever strikes your fancy that I can incorporate into my altar. By the way, it's my left breast, the one over my heart. Seems appropriate, right? I will also appreciate your prayers and moral support.

Love,
Hollis

December 5

Diagnosis: Infiltrating lobular carcinoma. Pronounced Friday, November 30.

Today I drove to the gated entrance to the compound where I live, punched in the code and waited. Nothing happened. Irritated, I began to punch in the code again and realized I was punching in the code to my storage facility, not my home.

At breakfast with Jeanne, I ordered my food, then asked the waitress what kind of milk would come with that. She looked puzzled. "Do you have 2 percent, or low fat?" I asked. "We don't usually serve milk with yogurt," she replied slowly. "Yogurt? I didn't order yogurt," I said. The waitress and Jeanne looked certain. "Yes, you did," they said in tandem. I'm sure my mouth was agape. I'd meant granola, not yogurt. I would never order yogurt in a restaurant.

I'm calling these "distraction reactions." And I recognize them as classic symptoms of grief; my "autopilot" function is disengaged. I know about grief, from my own past experiences and from my work as a hospital and hospice chaplain. I saw in that moment at the restaurant that I am in mourning—for my health, for the physical part of me I may lose and for the illusion of immortality.

Today the social worker at the clinic, a kind and thoughtful woman, presented Medicaid to me as a sort of consolation prize: "The bad news is you've got cancer. The good news is now you'll have full coverage Medicaid, and you can get dental, vision, even counseling!" No doubt she intended to cheer me up. "Your treatment without coverage could cost $100,000 or even $200,000!"

So I am lucky to be broke. If I had earned more than $28,000 last year or had health insurance, I would not get this coverage and could not pay for my treatment or co-pays. Our medical system is so broken. I am grateful to be "broker" than ever before in my life. Who ever thought I'd say that?

Looking back: When I arrived back here in Santa Fe in April, I was very sick with a virus. In the ensuing months I suffered great grief over the many changes in my life: the loss of relationship, loss of career, change of job, moving three times in nine months, loss of financial security.... I slept sometimes 10 hours a night, drank too much, lost 10 pounds between April and October. Were those signs of the cancer, causes or effects, or both? In June I took an online version of a classic psychological stress assessment based on life events and scored in the highest bracket, which prognosticated, "You have a nine in 10 chance of developing a serious illness within the next 12 months." As I mused about what illness I would be most susceptible to (but assuming this didn't apply to me, sort of like reading a bad horoscope), breast cancer came to mind. Prescient? Maybe.

The morning I found my lump, I awoke with a voice in my head saying, "You have a lump in your left breast." And I was feeling my breast in my sleep. I have never done self-exams because they seemed pointless, at least for me. My breasts are so dense and lumpy they've always felt like bags of marbles, and I've never been able to discern much. So the voice in my head, the lump my fingers felt, was such an extraordinary experience that I knew I had to get to the doctor. I knew, in fact, that it was cancer.

Other synchronicities and numinous incidents have happened. The morning I got the diagnosis, I awoke with the notion that my friend Dorothy would come over for our planned hike and the doctor would call with the news I had cancer and I would say, "Dorothy, let's go on our hike." And that was exactly what happened. I was showing Dorothy my courtyard when the phone rang. It was the radiologist with the bad news. Dorothy said, "What do you want to do?" and I said, "Let's go for our walk!" We had an amazing talk that morning.

Last spring, when I was trying to find a job in California, I decided I really just wanted to come home to Santa Fe. The three and a half years I had spent there—attending seminary and working as a chaplain resident in a hospital—had been wonderful, but the

Bay Area wasn't home. I felt that, if nothing else, I had a support system in Santa Fe. I decided if I were my own therapist, I'd say, "Go back to the Land of Enchantment, Hollis!" Little did I know what a great support system I had or how much I would need it. Three friends have offered to go to doctors' appointments with me when Jennifer can't. Each have had their own medical problems and nurtured other friends through theirs. I am so lucky.

Cancer Journal

December 12

What do I call this? My "illness" sounds so chronic—and possibly about some mental derangement that threatens to erupt at any moment. "The cancer" sounds dissociative, and I'm not sure I could say it aloud without laughing, since my sister and I have joked for years about people who use an article in front of a disease like an honorific. ("My cousin Rupert? He's got The Diabetes.") "The tumor" or even "my tumor" smacks of denial to me. It's not just a tumor; it's a condition whose extent we can only guess at right now (or perhaps ever, with our primitive diagnostic tools). I can't hear myself using a pejorative like "the beast" or even "the thing."

This is me, part of me, some kind of natural response of my body to external and internal stressors, possibly influenced by the environment and genetics, which has resulted in what I consider to be an imbalance that must be rectified. But neither can I hear myself saying, "Yes, I've had to change everything because of this imbalance." That, too, sounds like denial, or like I'm some woo-woo New Age disciple who's going to be drinking my own urine and standing on my head for an hour daily. So maybe I should give it a name, just an ordinary name—Herb, maybe. Or Alvin. It does seem so *male*. Howard? That's it. Meet my lump, Howard.

Distraction reaction: I left an hour ahead of an appointment instead of 30 minutes and thus found myself wasting precious time sitting in a parking lot.

Cancer Journal

December 13

Yesterday, a nurse at the surgeon's office called and informed me we needed to set up an appointment with yet another specialist: the radiation oncologist.

"No one's even told me I'll be having radiation," I said, though I had read online that it was a likely protocol for my kind of cancer.

"Oh, yes, we always have radiation after lumpectomy," she said. Always? Really? And what's this "we" business? Is she coming with me?

I feel like I am on a driverless bus, packed in with lots of other hot, sweaty, irritable folks, going somewhere we've never been before, no one speaking to anyone else, no one doing anything to stop the bus or even guide it. (The "hot and sweaty" no doubt comes from my hot flashes, which have returned with a vengeance since doctors found the tumor and I was told to stop—cold turkey— the hormone replacement therapy I was on.) So, next week: Radiation oncologist and surgeon. All before Christmas.

The bus reminds me of some lines from Naomi Shihab Nye's poem, "Kindness," which we used in a grief group I co-facilitated in Berkeley:

> *...How you ride and ride*
> *thinking the bus will never stop,*
> *the passengers eating maize and chicken will stare*
> *out the window forever.*
> *Before you learn*
> *the tender gravity of kindness,*
> *you must travel*
> *where the Indian in a white poncho*
> *lies dead by the side of the road.*
> *You must see how this could be you...*

I spoke to another nurse from the surgeon's office yesterday. I had emailed her to ask about my surgery and how soon afterward I can go back to work and whether or not I would be intubated (put on a breathing machine), as I assumed, during surgery. I can go back to work as soon as I feel up to it, she said, but should probably give myself the weekend after the Wednesday surgery and go back on Monday. One online source said you could go back to work the next day after a lumpectomy. Excuse me, but aren't we forgetting ourselves, our feelings, those unconscious responses we don't recognize? General anesthesia and slicing open my boob and armpit are no small things! Compared to a colectomy or heart surgery, this is a minor surgery, but all surgery is a big deal to the person having it. I felt so raw, so vulnerable, so invaded after the needle biopsy that I intend to honor myself and my body before and after this surgery. What has our health-care system come to when we say things like, "It's only a lumpectomy"?

Booby Blog #2

December 13

Dear Family and Friends,

I have been called on the carpet for not sending an update on my health since the first announcement of my breast cancer diagnosis. Who knew my Booby Blog would be so popular? (I actually thought about just posting these notes on my website, but unlike a lot of 20-somethings, I don't want *everyone* knowing all about my personal journey!)[1]

So, My Left Breast is becoming very well known in the Santa Fe community. Seems like everyone has met her, or wants to. Each day some nurse calls me to inform me that my next appointment will be with so-and-so, the such-and-such doctor. And I say, "Really? No one told me I'd be seeing him!" I called my friend Betty, who's had lots of medical experience. "Oh, yeah," she said knowingly. "Now you're in the queue. This is how it works. They'll just start telling you what to do."

Yesterday I had an MRI, which is supposed to provide more specific detail about what's going on in there. (It was strange: 35 minutes of lying on my stomach, with my boobs hanging out of holes in the table!) Right now, the tentative plan is a January 2 "lumpectomy with sentinel node biopsy," likely followed by radiation beginning a month after surgery. In the meantime, my life is a maelstrom of trying to keep up with my work as a part-time hospice chaplain—which is rather unpredictable, since death is unpredictable—and my work being my own medical case manager—which, as it turns out, is at least a half-time job, even at this point in the process. I have had to put most of my outside activities on hold for the moment.

---

1 Obviously, I changed my mind.

Thank you all for your calls and emails of support. Jennifer has been a great help already, going to appointments with me and cooking me yummy dinners. Three other friends have offered to go to appointments with me when she can't. I feel very loved and grateful to have so many wonderful people in my life.

Love,
Hollis

Cancer Journal

December 17

Lindy asked me, "How do you feel about your body?" and I told her instead what I don't feel: I don't feel any of those stereotypical media representations of cancer as The Enemy. I don't relate to the battlefield metaphors. I don't feel I need to "fight" the cancer. I feel the need to surrender to it instead. To accept it. To consider how my life has been out of balance and this, perhaps, is the result.

It's a fine line; I don't believe I "did this to myself" by any means, but my body has done something potentially self-destructive, perhaps entirely randomly—but if I had not gone through so much stress in the past few years, if I'd been taking somewhat better care of myself, perhaps my body could have resisted the disease response. I will never know the truth about that, if there is such a thing. Maybe that is the point—to find meaning, to make meaning for myself out of this, I must find a central truth.

I am reading Jean Shinoda Bolen's book, *Close to the Bone*, and she beautifully describes the process of *Life-Threatening Illness as a Soul Journey* (the subtitle). But I kept feeling something was missing, and finally realized it's that she is writing from the position of being outside looking in. She did not have a life-threatening illness but is writing as a physician and psychiatrist about that process. I need to read something by women with this illness or go to a support group for them.[2] I'll look in the paper today.

A friend came over today. She has had breast cancer—at least that was my understanding—but when I asked her about it, she said, "Oh, I was never told I have breast cancer. Just calcium deposits." And yet she had lumpectomies on both breasts, following diagnostic biopsies. I was puzzled. Later she added, "They said it was 'lobular carcinoma in situ.' " Now, this woman is really smart.

---

2 I had not yet identified myself as one of "them."

I know she knows "carcinoma" and "cancer" are the same thing. But somehow, her mind's path to protecting her has been to refuse to name it. Isn't that amazing? You could call that denial, but some studies show that people who don't acknowledge the severity or reality of their diseases live longer than people who do! Maybe her path, odd as it seems to me, is the right one for her.

Jennifer is going over the top caring for me. She has been fixing lots of meals, shopping, and buying me presents—big presents. Yesterday she got me the latest iPad, an expensive cover for it with a keyboard and a pair of pajamas. I worry that all this excess will result in resentment on her part. I mean, c'mon, does getting cancer entitle me to special treatment? That's crazy. I know she loves me, but I do try to admonish her not to go overboard. So far it has done no good.

Yet I do feel entitled, in an odd way. When I had a go-round with my boss this week, I said—as an excuse in part—"You know, I'm on a short tether these days," to which she replied, "All the more reason to take a deep breath before speaking." (I had snapped off at a meeting.) I wanted to say, "How dare you presume to know what I should or shouldn't do? I have cancer, my brain is not working well, I'm crying once an hour, my anxiety about money and the next medical procedure and whether or not I'm going to die are through the roof. So if I snap off once in a while, live with it." I didn't say any of that. But it is making me think seriously about whether I can continue to do my job through this.

$\mathcal{B}ooby \, \mathcal{B}log$ #3

December 17

Dear Ones,

This morning I had a second needle biopsy to see if there is a second tumor in my left breast. The results should be back by Thursday, when I see the surgeon again before my January 2 surgery. I also see the oncologist and the radiation oncologist and the underwater basket-weaving adviser—oh, wait, no, she's *next* week. Sorry, just kidding. These appointments are a trip! Who knew that this illness would give me wonderful time with the dear friends who have volunteered to be my moral supporters/record keepers at meetings? This week Jennifer, Mary and Marilyn are on tap.

I am so grateful to have so many caring friends. Thank you all for your moral support and for the sweet cards, emails and images you have sent. I moved household this week, so I am just now getting my altar set up again.[3] Once I think it looks photo-worthy, I'll send an image of it to you all.

Thank goodness I finished my holiday gift buying and mailing early. No cards are going out, but at least through this I am in touch with you all.

Love,
Hollis

---

3 After discovering my cancer—which coincided with learning that the place I'd been living would soon no longer be available—my girlfriend, Jennifer, generously offered to share her home with me.

Booby Blog #4

December 19

Dear Ones:

The good news is in! The second area the docs were worried might be cancerous has turned out to be benign, so I need only tangle with "Howard." Yesterday I got to spend about four hours with my dear friend Marilyn, who accompanied me to two new doc appointments—the oncologist and the radiation oncologist. Much of the time was spent in waiting rooms and in exam rooms. We behaved like teenagers called to the principal's office, talking and giggling and having a good time overall. At one point, Marilyn asked, "Just how many people have touched that boob since all this started, anyway?"

Let's see: two mammogram techs, three ultrasound techs, one MRI tech, three radiologists, my primary doc, the oncologist, the radiation oncologist, the janitor—oh, no, he doesn't count, I guess—so...12. I'm thinking there's a song in this, to the tune of "The Twelve Days of Christmas," perhaps!

Today it's snowing and beautiful, which means I get to stay at home and do computer work all day. Tomorrow I see the surgeon again and, hopefully, we'll get the surgery details decided.

Thank you all for your support.

Love,
Hollis

Booby Blog #5

December 22

Dear Beloved Ones:

It's almost Christmas, and I get several consecutive days with no doctors' appointments or procedures (at least as far as I know)! This does not mean a hall pass, however; I have much to think about.

Jennifer spent an hour and a half with me at the surgeon's office on Thursday. I did not anticipate having *choices* about the surgery; somehow I thought it would all be fairly clear-cut, but alas, that's not the case. So now I am hearing the *Jeopardy* theme song in my head as I ponder, on my 10-day time limit (surgery is currently set for January 2), whether to have a lumpectomy or a mastectomy. It's all very complicated.

In the meantime, I've made a huge decision on another front: I've quit my part-time position as a hospice chaplain for the time being. I've found that no amount of stoicism or prayer will allow me to sit with a dying patient and/or family members and be completely present to their needs while the *Jeopardy* song is occupying my brain. The company and my colleagues are completely supportive, and it's entirely possible I can go back to it when this—this what? phase of my life?—is over. I was thinking about what quitting my job represents, and the TV slogan that popped to mind was the old bra commercial touting "no visible means of support!" I'm afraid that all the metaphors my mind dredges up these days are bad booby jokes. I could not have made this decision without the encouragement of my spiritual advisers, for whom I am extremely grateful.

So, between now and the 28th, I'll be wrapping up my work for the hospice company and sitting with the decisions I have to make. Thank God for Jennifer, who is being endlessly supportive in every way. She's treating me to a four-day retreat at a B&B in southern Colorado after Christmas.

I wish you and yours a fabulous holiday season full of laughter, music, good food, great friends and loving family!

Love,
Hollis

Booby Blog #6

January 1

Dear Friends and Family:

[Note to newcomers: This is my Booby Blog, the serial email by which I'm keeping my peeps apprised of my challenge with breast cancer. Welcome to the fray! Graphic content is always a possibility.][4]

Tomorrow's the day that "Howard," as I've affectionately dubbed my tumor, gets the boot! For those of you following this story, I ultimately decided to opt for a lumpectomy rather than a mastectomy at this stage of the game. It's a much simpler, outpatient surgery, though I will have a few procedures in advance so the "day surgery" process will really take all day, from about 8 a.m. until 4 p.m. or so. This will be the longest fast of my life to date, I think, except when I've had the stomach flu!

The outpouring of support I have received from all of you has been tremendous, and I truly appreciate it. I've been reading a fabulous book recommended by Katy, a friend who is a breast cancer survivor. It's called *Anticancer: A New Way of Life*, by David Servan-Schreiber, M.D., Ph.D. It's about how we must change our lifestyles, eating habits and psychospiritual self-care to prevent and recover from cancer—good advice for everyone (and a surprisingly great read).

Servan-Schreiber notes that the Nurses' Health Study, the largest-scale long-term study of women's health ever undertaken in the United States, showed that "women with breast cancer who could name ten friends had a four times better chance of surviving their illness than women who could not. The geographic proxim-

---

4 From this missive forward, I always included a disclaimer like this one.

ity of those friendships was not significant; the protective effect seemed to stem from the simple fact of feeling connected."

What greater reassurance could I ask for? There are currently 58 of you on this list, 58 people (who live all over the country) who truly care about me and my well-being.[5] Thank you for supporting me through this part of my journey. Some days I've felt as if I was on a raft in the midst of the rapids, but all of you have been running along the riverbank holding ropes attached to my raft, keeping me stable, afloat and tethered to the shore. And a three-day retreat to a beautiful B&B near Durango, Colorado, with Jennifer has calmed the waters substantially. We watched a pair of nesting bald eagles in a tree at roadside; a wild turkey ran across the highway in front of us; and we hiked in deep, sparkling snow through fields of sagebrush bounded by snowcapped mountains. Life doesn't get much better than that.

Tomorrow, Jennifer and Mimi will be with me at the hospital. My dear friend and chaplain-mentor Penny has recorded a prayer on my voicemail for me to listen to in the morning. Lori, a medical hypnotherapist recommended by another friend, has created a recording I will listen to during my surgery on my iPod. And I trust all of you will be thinking of me and sending me healing energy tomorrow and in the coming weeks.

Thank you! More to come, soon.

Love,
Hollis

---

5 The list eventually grew to approximately 80 friends and family members.

Booby Blog #1

January 3

Dear Ones:

All is well. Howard has departed for the pathology lab, and I am snuggled in bed in new button-front jammies from my mom, with the iPhone, iPad, noise-canceling headphones and my brand-new 2013 journal at my side. They will probably all go unused for the time being. Sleep is calling.

Jennifer and I left here at 7:45 a.m. yesterday, and I was not home in bed until that time last night because the operating room was running *hours* behind schedule. Thank goodness I had Jennifer and Mimi to sit with me. We talked our heads off and laughed a good deal, and by the time they finally came to wheel me in, all anxiety had dissipated. Adding to the normally curious qualities of pre-op (familiar to me from my chaplaincy residency days) was the fact that directly across the hall was an old friend of mine from media days gone by—having exactly the same surgery as I! And the friend who was attending her was a former boss of mine from my newspaper days. We eavesdropped on each other until eventually my old boss came over for a chat. Only in a small town, eh?

Jennifer and Mimi were saints and never lost their senses of humor as the waiting dragged on and on and on. Since I was not allowed food or water from midnight forward, I was edging toward cranky by late afternoon, which prompted Jennifer to ask, "Hey, how about some chocolate? Cake? What can I get you?" Today she is busy checking my wound, feeding me pain pills, tending my ice bag and the like. This is her second experience of late as Nurse Nancy, but I daresay she's come up in the world; last time around, tending her friend Edith, she had only hospital-issue green latex gloves. But I had my own stash, thanks to my former employer, and can I just say she looks much better in hot *pink* latex?

Thank you all for your support, emails, calls and offers of help. And now, to sleep.

Love,
Hollis

P.S. At my post-op appointment with the surgeon next Tuesday, I will get the lowdown on Howard, recommended treatments, prognosis, etc.

Cancer Journal

January 4

Surgery was two days ago. A long day that began at 7:45, and I wasn't home until 7:45 p.m. Bad scheduling—long waits between pre-op procedures—then a long delay to get into surgery. Mimi and Jennifer were with me the whole time. Yesterday I slept most of the day and today slept most of the morning. Did not feel good at all—sleepy, depressed—and listened to numerous meditation CDs (including Lori's special recording for me and one other generic one she had created) on the noise-canceling headphones Jennifer gave me. But, ultimately, I had to take some more Percocet to feel well enough to move around.

Jeanne and I talked of this before my surgery—how docs always describe recovery as if it were no big deal. I have actually been in quite a bit of pain and very woozy from painkillers. One must remember that, in most cases, the physician has not had this surgery, and he or she has been through it vicariously with hundreds of patients, thus diminishing any sense of what a shock it is to the body and psyche.

If I were Osiris (an ancient Egyptian god with whom I have an affinity), then I have arrived at the point in the myth at which I have been killed and dismembered by my brother Set—before the point at which Isis recovers all my parts and puts me back together. What must I do to effect that healing?

Cancer Journal

January 6

Yesterday, I spent much more time up—most of the day, in fact—and did more arm exercises and the like. Madeline's friend Janine—who has had two mastectomies and at one point was told she would die within three months (that was a decade ago!)—told me a lot about her experience and reinforced the need for exercising the arm on the surgery side to prevent lymphedema and for physical therapy later.

But the day started with Jennifer helping me take a shower. I was able to stand and do most of the bathing myself, but she dried me off, put lotion on me and helped me dress. I started crying as she dressed me—I felt so humbled and vulnerable. I am crying now just remembering it. It was so hard to accept my dependency.

I need to make my recovery plan, which I don't yet have. I guess the truth is that it will evolve. Maybe I will use another notebook for that. So far, I have a regimen of anti-cancer, anti-inflammatory herbs and homeopathic remedies recommended by a doctor of Oriental medicine and a nutritionist. Two times a day of that stuff. Food: I am already eating better. I cut out caffeinated coffee and switched to decaf. I am having Ceylon cinnamon in my coffee—an anti-cancer spice, supposedly. I am drinking green tea three times a day. I am eating more multicolored veggies and no sugar (although honey in some things and some sweets, I admit). I need to find a meditation group where I can just show up and sit. Sounds like a full-time job, and maybe it is for a while. Hard not to feel guilty and worried about that; how will I survive financially?

Today I must deal with my car, which will not go. The battery is dead, my intuition suggested yesterday, and it was right.

Cancer Journal

January 7

My boob feels so weird. I have sensations like electrical shocks or stabbing sensations to my nipple, then feelings like vibrations in my tissue that radiate toward the nipple. The wounds themselves don't seem to hurt. I read somewhere that these weird feelings can last up to two years after surgery. (And yet, we are to believe it is not a big deal. Right.)

Last night I was able to lie on my stomach in bed for a while. But I also had terrible chills and could not get warm and had to get Jennifer to get the little portable room heater and extra blankets. It took a long time to warm up. Then in the morning at 2 or 3 a.m. I awoke with terrific night sweats—hot, then cold, hot, then cold.

Tomorrow, surgeon. Stitches out. News of pathology.

Also struck by our Western medicine system of specialization. I asked my primary doctor some questions I thought were pretty basic about cancer, and she deferred to the oncologist. I asked the oncologist about radiation, and she deferred to the radiation oncologist—although I had wanted her opinion because she is not a radiation oncologist and might therefore be less biased. My perception is that the state of Western medicine is utterly barbaric and broken. Nothing about it makes sense.

Cancer Journal

January 9

Yesterday saw the surgeon. I took off my shirt, and she looked at me from three feet away and said it looked great. (Turns out these are all dissolving stitches. Nothing to remove.) Then we proceeded to talk results, all good: Stage 1, Grade 1, caught as early as possible, really, and the margins around the primary area of the cancer were clear, as they say. I asked if she would have my tissue tested—there's a test for the potential of recurrence—and she said she had been about to suggest that. I asked for a copy of the final report, and she handed me the one she held, having anticipated that, too.

But I felt odd, and later, on reflection, realized that despite her kind and caring demeanor, I felt something was off, and it was: She didn't touch me during this "exam" or after. A hand on the shoulder or arm, an arm around my side in a half-hug as I left—any or all would have transmitted caring in a way that engenders trust, even belief, in the physicians' power to engage in co-healing with the patient. I know health caregivers are very careful about touching patients who may not want to be touched, but with some attuning to body language and conversation, you'd think that would usually be clear enough. And surely she could risk some physical contact, since she's a woman doctor seeing patients who are almost exclusively female.

I held out my hand to shake hers when I left and discovered she is one of those people who offers a limp hand for you to hold. So perhaps she is uncomfortable with physical contact or shy of connection that isn't purely clinical. Maybe that's why she became a surgeon rather than an internist; surely among surgeons technical expertise, artistry even, is privileged over compassion and connection. Even so, I found it odd she didn't touch the breast she'd recently sliced into, just to check her handiwork. It made me feel like a pariah.

Booby Blog #8

January 9

Dear Loved Ones:

Good news! Yesterday I saw the surgeon for a one-week follow-up and got the results of the pathology testing: There's no evidence of cancer in the lymph nodes, and the margins were clear,
meaning that the tiny samples of tissue taken from around the area
of the primary tumor showed up negative for cancer. "Howard"
truly has departed. All of this data give me a "score" of Stage 1/
Grade 1 invasive lobular cancer. All of which means my prognosis
is very bright.

I am awaiting results of another lab test that is predictive of
recurrence. Today I see the oncologist about follow-up treatment
(more tough decisions!) and another doctor who is stuffing me full
of anti-cancer supplements (which Medicaid does not cover).

My only complaint now is that, as you might suspect, my
breast and left underarm (where they removed lymph nodes) are
still swollen and painful. Some of the articles I read before this
surgery said you could go back to work the next day. "And in just a
few days, you'll feel fine." *Really?* Who makes this stuff up? In one
of the least fun pre-surgery procedures, a radiologist injected my
breast with radioactive dye. The male tech had predicted it would
feel "like a TB test." I involuntarily yelped, "Shit!" out loud when
the doc did the injection. It was *very* painful. Why didn't they dead-
en the breast, as they had for biopsies, I asked? "Well, then you'd
have to have two shots," the doc replied. "Let me tell you," I said,
"the lidocaine shot is a bee sting compared to that one." As I left
the department, I couldn't resist saying to the tech, "How would
you feel if you had a needle stuck in *your* most sensitive body part?"
They'd have to give men a general anesthetic! (Sorry, guys.)

Thank you all for your wonderful cards, emails, phone calls and gifts, and thanks especially to those of you who have been giving up your time to accompany me to the appointments. I deeply appreciate it all. I have felt loved and supported through all of this.

Love,
Hollis

Cancer Journal

January 10

Yesterday was the first post-surgical visit to the oncologist, Dr. Jasper. Dorothy was supposed to accompany me, but she was sick, so Jennifer did. I have been musing about the oncologist. Ideally, I would have someone who was an M.D. and D.O.M. (Doctor of Oriental Medicine) or other kind of alternative practitioner who does what they call "integrative" or "complementary" medicine. Dr. Jasper, I guessed, does not, and a friend of a friend in the same situation as I am said she found her "rigid." So yesterday, when she repeated the same "radiation-plus-aromatase-inhibitors-for-five-years" protocol—despite my Stage 1/Grade 1/clear margins surgical outcome, I attempted (with Jennifer's help) to ask about alternative solutions.

Her answer—for example, about the potential terrible side effects of aromatase inhibitors—was, over and over again, "We can give you medications to help you deal with that," or, "We will monitor you closely for that." She had no suggestions for lifestyle or nutrition changes. She suggested anti-depressants for menopause symptoms and said yoga and acupuncture could help alleviate symptoms during aromatase inhibitor therapy. She wrote an order for me to have acupuncture there in the cancer clinic but had no idea about payment: "It depends on your insurance." One more way in which the healer is separated from the patient, as if talking about money or even knowing the patient's financial situation was somehow verboten or shameful.

As luck would have it, the woman at the front desk had me fill out an application for funding from the hospital's foundation and said they would pay for six acupuncture sessions.

Somehow, I keep getting what I need today. In the end, I asked Jennifer what she thought of Dr. Jasper. "I liked her," she said. So do I, even though she can only help me in her own very limited way. I am the designer of my own recovery, and all patients today should know that they must take responsibility for their own healing to achieve the best results. No one else can do it for you. No more Marcus Welby, M.D. (Heck, no Dr. House, for that matter! Though his bedside manner sucks, at least he is intensely devoted to the unique medical problem of the individual patient.)

If I were a patient advocate, that's what I would tell people: No matter how sick you are, no matter that this is the most difficult challenge of your life, you must captain your own ship. You must get all the help you can from family, friends, and health-care practitioners, but ultimately, you must take responsibility for yourself. (Of course, the sickest of us can't, in which case their loved ones must do for them what they cannot do for themselves.)

Last night I worked four and a half hours sorting through tax documents for Jennifer. She is paying me for the work. But I stood for so long that my back was killing me, along with my still-swollen and tender boob. It will be a long time before I can run again, I know. It's just been a week, but I am anxious to get moving.

Cancer Journal

January 15

It's been almost two weeks since surgery. Immediately afterward, I had the sense that "it" was gone, but I also felt motivated to change. I notice in myself now a loss of that special motivation—and that seems dangerous. I could go back to being the "old" me with my old ways and bring back the cancer. It seems I may need to guard against "backsliding." It's not really that I am not doing as I should. I am still eating well and taking my supplements and reading (now *Cancer As a Turning Point: A Handbook for People With Cancer, Their Families, and Health Professionals* by Lawrence LeShan, which the author of *Anticancer* quoted from extensively). Just a subtle shift inside that I sense I must pay attention to. What can I do today to support my new awareness? Something about beauty—bringing more beauty into my life. So far, seeking out beauty has not been among the things I've read that people with cancer should do to recover and mend their lives, but I know it is essential to my healing.

Cancer Journal

January 16

Yesterday I went for acupuncture, and the D.O.M. gave me an additional Chinese medicine tonic to take in hot water three times a day. Plus she wants me to do a green drink, plus dandelion root tea, added to all the other stuff the nutritionist has put me on, and the mushroom capsules another D.O.M. friend of a friend recommended, and the things I believe I should take. I'm taking perhaps 15 things twice a day. And she suggested doing a "cleanse" for three to five days once a month. I just don't believe my body needs all of this—seems it might be confused, in fact (as am I). Are we just bombarding it with supplements and hoping something works? Each practitioner has his or her own theories, and most (although not all) make money on the sale of these things. How do I sort it out?

The *Anticancer* book talked about food, not supplements. Perhaps I should find a book that addresses those particularly for breast cancer. Next on the agenda after I finish what I'm reading now.

Booby Blog #9

January 18

Dear Ones:

As I sit here drinking my noxious-tasting Shen Qi Wan/Dau Shen (dissolved in green tea), I am struck by what I think of as my higher power's sense of humor. You know how people love to say, "Watch what you ask for—you might get it"? There's a corollary: "Watch what you laugh at—you'll soon be doing it." Much of my life I have privately rolled my eyes and snickered at people who are obsessed with their health, buy every new supplement that Dr. Oz or Dr. Weil suggests and forever seem to be seeing a new health-care practitioner of some kind or another.

And now? *This is my life.* I (who can barely get a pill down) am currently taking 20 different supplements, vitamins and prescription drugs (some multiple times a day, and some are two pills each time). It's sobering to think that the kitchen or bathroom counter of probably everyone who has a severe or chronic illness looks like mine. That is, everyone who can afford this stuff. I won't even go into the dietary changes and all the other things I am doing in an effort to boost my immune system and restore my health.

With that in mind, I am practicing gratitude for all these pills and all the people who are telling me to take them. One of the things I am taking is a flower essence called Blue Pentangle prescribed by my nutritionist. It comes with its own affirmation: "I am competent." The nutritionist suggested I say, "I am competent to meet this challenge." Trust me, there is no eye rolling or snickering going on now.

My wounds are healing well, though I still have some pain. I was able to put on a real bra and took my first walk yesterday since the surgery. Yay! On January 29, I will get the results of the genome test that predicts risk of recurrence, which will help me make decisions about other recommended treatments.

I am so lucky and grateful. What are you grateful for today?

Love,
Hollis

Cancer Journal

January 19

Yesterday I started writing down everything I eat, take or do that I associate with my healing process. Jennifer had given me a little green notebook—the kind with an elastic band to close it, which I love—and I chose it to be my "healing journal." She also gave me a larger purple one, the one I'm writing in now, which has a purple satin ribbon for a place marker. This one I consider more of a diary, a narrative, of my feelings and impressions of this process. Somehow I felt this event, or situation, deserved its own special journal.

But back to the little green book. What is it about writing things down that seems to make them more real to me? It's almost as if I have—in Joan Didion's words—"magical thinking" going on—as if, by chronicling all I am doing to be healthy, it will "prove" to Whoever Is in Charge that I am worthy of healing. And perhaps prove to myself that I am doing all that is possible—following all the "rules," so to speak. It seems akin to the "bargaining" phase of grief, in the Elisabeth Kübler-Ross paradigm, the hope of postponing or delaying death. Bargaining with the Unknown!

Well, at least it does not hurt me to do these things, and it may indeed help me keep up with all the things I should do or at least try in this "anti-cancer" effort. But possibly the most important thing to do is the "inside job," some shift in my thinking. I have seen some inklings of this as I go through my days and will hopefully encounter more to come.

Cancer Journal

January 20

Awoke this morning with a pain in my left eye. Got up, put the dogs out, started the coffee and thought, wow, that hurts—oh! I should go look in the mirror. The outside half of my left eye is deep, bloody red—a hemorrhage! It hurts with each blink. My first thoughts were catastrophic. #1: It's brain cancer! There is a tumor in my brain. I've probably had some kind of stroke in my sleep! #2: It's probably the unconventional treatments I'm taking. My supplements caused this. (In other words, I'm breaking the "rules," and here is the proof and the punishment!)

So, I did what any good codependent, overly responsible person would do: I prepared for the emergency room. I began packing a bag with books and journals and all my supplements and started planning how to get backup dog care in case I got stuck there, since Jennifer is out of town. I also started crying but made myself stop because I knew it would make my eye worse. I thought about which friends I could call to come be with me and felt bereft of friends—I, who have 60-plus people on her Booby Blog, people I know care about me deeply! Not all of them are the type who could handle an E.R. run, but certainly some are and would be glad to help out.

Then I broke down and called Jennifer for a reality check. She would want to support me and, if I did not call, would surely ask me why I didn't. I also started looking up "blood in the eye" on the Internet as I dialed her. She was reassuring and loving as always. She's had one of these bloody eyes herself, and so had a friend of hers, she said, and all the news online was good: It was likely a subconjunctival hemorrhage, caused by a big cough, sneeze, choking, straining (even from constipation, though that is never my problem!) and possibly—drum roll, please—flatulence! Well, though I am the queen of farting, I could not recall any earth-shattering, high-decibel toots in the last 24 hours. What I did recall was the terrific strain of opening the garage-style door on my storage space yesterday and, to spare my left side, doing it all with my right—much harder than when both sides are working. That effort seems the likely cause, although it was yesterday afternoon when that occurred, meaning a delayed reaction.

According to the websites, it will take a few days to a few weeks for this to go away.[6] Jennifer suggested I go visit our friend Edith today; after all, she is a Harvard-trained nurse practitioner. I think I will take it easy, be with the dogs, cook, watch a movie. Take a day off. I am always telling Jennifer to do this. My argument for a day off is always that the work will still be there in a day, and I will feel better and therefore be more efficient and centered to do it if I will give myself a "Sabbath." So I will.

---

6 It was eight weeks before it totally disappeared.

Booby Blog #10

January 24

Dear Ones:

Did you hear me whoop and holler from wherever you live? Yes, it's true, I have finally been able to shave under the arm where they removed some lymph nodes! It was getting so bad they wouldn't have let me on a lesbian cruise. Another first: The last ring of the shower curtain fell off the rod this morning, and I was able to reach up and replace it without busting something open. We need to celebrate our small successes, right?

This experience is teaching me so much; every day I hear an echo of something I learned in seminary or chaplaincy training or something I have heard myself tell patients in the hospital or hospice. I am my own patient now.

For example: On Sunday I got a subconjunctival hemorrhage (a bloody eye) and decided I was probably dying. But another part of my brain, my witnessing mind, was saying, "*Oh*. This is what happens when you have a chronic or serious disease. Everything becomes evidence of it, another reason to be afraid, another sign that you are probably going to die—and probably sooner than you think."

Later, my friend Dorothy, who walked with her husband to his death from cancer years ago, confirmed that "catastrophizing" response. While her husband was sick, any little thing that went wrong terrorized them, she said. We don't just "catastrophize"or "awfulize" when we are sick. Some of us do it when we are perfectly well. I certainly do!

And this morning, another feeling crept in that I recognized as a common response to grief when someone has died and some time has passed. It's a feeling I know many of you reading this have experienced, too. As I was sorting through my passel of supplements and making my blueberry-pomelo-yogurt breakfast, I idly thought, Well, this has been very instructive, but when do I get my *real* life back? The answer is the one I have told my patients: "You don't. But you're going to get a 'new normal.' It just takes time."

Thanks for listening!

Love,
Hollis

Cancer Journal

January 25

I wrote Booby Blog #5 about catastrophizing—thinking every little health event is a sign it's back or has spread. At the same time, I often feel I am blowing this whole thing out of proportion. After all, I had the surgery, the lump is gone, it all looks good. Shouldn't I just be moving on, for goodness' sake? It's my own personal inner critic, who shuts down my feelings, demands stoicism, tells me that I and my life are no big deal, not special, not unique. I'll be boring people if I keep going on with this cancer stuff.

But nowadays, some other inner force—one that I truly believe has my best interests at heart—is saying, "This is the only life you have, and you are, in fact, the star of this movie. So act like you are." Keep the focus on me, in other words. Jean Shinoda Bolen said that she had learned to discern what to do in times of indecision by asking, "What is in my best interests?" (I'm paraphrasing here.) This is a time in my life when I must unabashedly make those choices, choices for me. I already have been saying no a lot to things I don't want to do.

A few other random thoughts: I realized the other day that I was thinking of this cancer as being somehow contained in my breast or only related to my breast. Our language encourages that; it is "breast cancer," after all. But, in fact, it is an aberration of normal cell growth that happened to find purchase in my breast, and the cells match what Western/allopathic medicine calls breast cancer. But somehow limiting my view of it to a certain body part seems counterintuitive and even counterproductive to my healing. We know so little about the mechanism of cancer; we don't know why it's in my breast instead of my skin or my brain, for example. Why did I get cancer, and why is it in my breast? It seems so important to treat my whole self—body and soul—not just my breast.

Cancer Journal

January 26

Awoke with depression. What if I do all the "right things" and I die anyway? I tried to say to myself, "Well, then, you'd better get busy!" As a balm, it didn't work. I still felt depressed. It's hard to make decisions. Should I go see this alternative doctor, Dr. Heller? I would have to pay her out of pocket. I've read her website, and, frankly, I'm not sure I believe in half the stuff she recommends.

I need to make some changes, that's for sure. Can I do it?

Ironically, Jennifer has been doing a cleanse, and a lot of the things that are recommended on this diet she already practices. And I have been very judgmental about her motivations and ideas. Seems things just keep coming back to bite me in the butt—and very quickly these days.

$$\mathcal{B}ooby\ \mathcal{B}log\ \#11$$

February 2

Dear Ones:

I am reminded this morning of how, in the Walker family, I was the kid who hated the roller coaster. I haven't been on one in probably 45 years, but these days my life seems to resemble one.

Last week I went to the oncologist with great anticipation of the results of the oncotypeDX™ test. This test uses your own cancerous breast tissue, taken during surgery, to analyze 21 genes and thereby predict your personal risk of recurrence of breast cancer. Or so I understood, from what I had read on the company's website and been told by my oncologist.

As it turns out, the test measures those genes in your tissue and compares them to the genes taken from cancer tissue of patients who had breast cancer and underwent Tamoxifen (estrogen-blocking) drug therapy for five years. Some of those patients subsequently got cancer somewhere else in their bodies ("distant cancer," it's called, what we generally think of as "metastasized.") Some of them didn't. The comparison of your genes and the genes of those studied produces a score that correlates to a percentage of risk of distant recurrence of cancer within 10 years. Got that?

According to this test, I have an eight percent risk of distant recurrence, *assuming* I take aromatase inhibitors (the estrogen-blockers that are similar to Tamoxifen and given to post-menopausal women). But the test doesn't distinguish among patients who also had radiation, or also had chemotherapy, or both. It isn't necessarily accurate for women who *don't* undergo aromatase inhibitor treatment. Still, it's the best predictor we've got.

But it's not the magic number I was hoping for. What I wanted to know was my personal overall risk of recurrence of cancer anywhere in my body, based on my unique makeup. Yet even if such a number could be clinically proven, it wouldn't matter. How does one quantify fear, or plan for outcomes, based on statistics? Maybe my risk of distant recurrence does fall (hallelujah) somewhere in the eight percent range—but what if I'm one of the eight percent? (And why the hell don't they express it in a positive way, e.g, "You have a 92 percent chance this cancer will not come back!")

During the discussion about this test with my oncologist, I explained that I wasn't at all sure I would do aromatase inhibitor therapy, because the side effects are quite serious and potentially life threatening, and I wasn't even certain I would do radiation (the next course of recommended action, slated to begin this month). At the last she looked askance and said, "Well, I can't imagine why not," and proceeded to speedily run down a checklist of every possible side effect of radiation and why I shouldn't worry about it, including statistics. When she was done, I really, really had to fight the urge to say, "Great! Since it's so safe, why don't you come along with me? Let's get a two-fer!" (I probably would have said it, but she's pregnant, and I thought that might come across as mean-spirited.)

So I'm going this week to get a second opinion from an on-cologist who has been recommended to me by numerous people. I really don't expect him to suggest anything different than what my current oncologist suggested, but a part of me is hoping for a slightly more *human* response. How hard would it have been for her to say, "Wow, sounds like you're really concerned about this. Let's talk about it." This wasn't the first time I've felt this way in my appointments with her, and I (the once-intrepid newspaper re-porter) find myself completely at a loss for words when it happens. What's the point of trying harder to engage her in conversation? She doesn't see me; she sees a number, a statistic, a *probability*, sit-ting in front of her.

I talked about this with my friend Joan, who has her own on-going health challenges. She's had the same kinds of experiences, so much so that she avoids seeing her doctors as much as possible. "They're just technocrats," she said. I was reminded of some of the brilliant young doctors I watched in action while working at Kaiser Medical Center in Vallejo, California. They ordered tests and wrote prescriptions with alacrity but almost never touched their patients except for necessary clinical examinations, and they often stood 10 feet from the bed while talking to them. They were indeed brilliant about the technical aspects of their profession but clueless about the art of healing. In contrast was a physician of retirement age who pulled up a chair next to his patients' beds, looked into their eyes and touched a shoulder or patted a hand in comfort while he talked with them. He was every patient's favorite hospitalist.

Joan loaned me a copy of Dr. Jerome Groopman's book *How Doctors Think*, which I highly recommend for anyone whose life intersects the medical world. Groopman uses case studies gathered from physicians to demonstrate how over-reliance on algorithms, technology and medical records causes them to misdiagnose, mistreat and sometimes even kill their patients. He also tells some amazing "rescue" stories, in which the heroes of the medical world are the doctors who actually pay attention to their patients, who listen, ask questions and collaborate with them. That's what I want, and that's what I'm going to keep asking for.

I'm afraid this became something of a rant. On a happier note, my incisions are completely healed; I've been walking more regularly; I am now able to lie on my tummy painlessly again; and—drum roll please—I can finally sleep without a bra on! (Guys: Sleeping in a bra may be the equivalent of sleeping in an athletic supporter. Just guessing.) *Life is good.*

Love,
Hollis

$Booby$ $Blog$ #12

February 14

Dear Ones:

No ranting today, I promise! The roller coaster has come to a halt, it seems. Or maybe it's just hit one of those low points, when the screaming has stopped and you can hear your own heartbeat slowing to normal—just before another terrifying ascent.

I signed on with Dr. Monroe, the oncologist I visited for a second opinion. He turned out, as predicted by those who recommended him, to be very warm, friendly and open-minded. As I suspected, he made the same recommendations as my previous oncologist, but he made a point of empowering me to make my own decisions. ("It's your body; it's really up to you," he said.)

The upshot of all this is I am beginning radiation next week. Yesterday I went for a "planning session," at which I had a CT scan and the technician wrote in hieroglyphs all over my chest with a fat black Sharpie (shouldn't there be some really *special* kind of marker for writing on human skin?) and then covered the marks with clear tape. Next week, at the final planning session, they'll mark me up with permanent tattoo dots, so each time they can aim the radiation to a pinpoint. I had thought that after one planning session I'd start right into radiation the next day. "Oh, no, this is very complicated," the tech told me, which had the amusing and paradoxical effect of reassuring me that they were taking it all very seriously—and making me a bit more nervous than I already was. What if they incorrectly enter an algorithm and fry my shoulder or left foot instead of my boob?

I also decided to see Dr. Heller, the M.D. who practices integrative medicine. She spent an hour and a half with me and gave me so many recommendations for diet, vitamins, supplements, exercise and other treatments that it's going to take me a while to adjust or at least to experiment with how far I can go (not to mention what I can afford). I'm afraid I will be a disappointment to her in some ways, as I know I will never quit eating all forms of sugar forever. "Of course not," said my friend Barbara. "Sugar is *life*!"

I'm going to have to approach this from the perspective of learning all over again how to shop, cook and eat—for example, discovering the joys of sprouted mung beans. My dietary CliffsNotes: no dairy, no soy, no milled grains (flour-based foods), no alcohol, no sugar. We had bison burgers, brown rice and baked squash last night for dinner, and waiting in the freezer is some grass-fed, free-range, no hormones or antibiotics, organic ground yak meat ($7.99 a pound) for another burger night in the near future. Woohoo!

Love,
Hollis

Cancer Journal

February 15

I realized I hadn't written much in here lately. Perhaps for a couple of reasons: I'm integrating Hollis-with-breast-cancer with plain old Hollis and writing my Booby Blog on topics closer to the bone; and/or I am just disidentifying with the cancer, as the surgery is over and I have fully recovered from it. But there is also an urge, sparked in part by discussions with other women who have had breast cancer, to diminish the whole thing.

Yesterday on the phone with my old friend Barbara, she seemed to do that, saying, "Well, if they catch it early, and you get it taken care of...." I could envision her brushing her hands together in that gesture of completion, good riddance, that's done. Doubt crept in: Maybe I'm just making a big deal out of this in order to have a drama in my life, an excuse to take it easy for a while. But no, I thought. This is a life-threatening disease. It is a wake-up call to my mortality, if nothing else, but also to see the potential for living in a healthier way, one that will improve my quality of life. My friend's reasons for saying what she did could be many. Maybe she is in denial about her situation and must shield herself against the thought of her mortality in order to go on. Or maybe she was just trying to say something she thought would reassure me. But as I thought about embracing that notion—it really isn't a big deal; I really can just move on—I realized in doing so I would be ignoring my own best advice, counsel I included in a recent sermon I did called "Choosing Transformation": You can't go backward. You can't push the rabbit back into the hat, the genie back into the bottle, the shoot back into the bulb. Once you have seen the truth or reality or even the magic of a situation, there can be no return to innocence or ignorance.

And now that I have glimpsed my own mortality, I cannot go back to believing that what I once thought mattered so much really does. Still, it is hard to sit with this knowing; it remains somewhat murky, and the "new" me doesn't know where she is going or how to get there or how to even pay the bills along the way. Sitting with this uncertainty and not doing anything right now is terribly hard. Every day my mind takes an excursion down "what if" lane, imagining poverty, homelessness, an old age alone in a dark garret or having to go live with my mother in Texas (I love Mom, and Texas has its assets, but that's not on my bucket list).

I have to remind myself that I am still in the middle of this transformation. What is called for now is not action but contemplation, prayer, meditation, writing and restoring my emotional, spiritual and physical health, no matter what.

I'm pleased that I've begun walking again. Today I hope to try a yoga class; I've found one that's cheap. And this evening, Jennifer and I will try for the first time the far-infrared sauna that Dr. Heller recommends for detoxification. Radiation begins next week. I am beginning to contemplate how I will make it a spiritual ritual. Thirty-four sessions.

I have neglected to record a few important things along the way. One day I spoke with my friend Candy on the phone. I had written her an email about my cancer. She has been facing her own health crisis and has been living mostly in isolation for the past year. One day Candy told me that her daughter Sheryl, whom I adore, had dreamed that a friend of theirs with light hair had breast cancer—but that she was now OK. When Sheryl (who has had psychic events all her life) awoke, she called her mother to tell her the dream and see if they could figure out who the "light-haired woman" was. I had told Candy about my cancer after my surgery, and it was shortly after that when Sheryl had the dream, which they now both believed was about me.

Then, in Taos, after I gave my sermon at the Unitarian Universalist Church a few weeks ago, a woman approached me to thank me. Indicating rather obliquely that she is a healer of some kind, she took me by both hands and said, "I know that you are well."

I think they are right.

Booby Blog #13

February 21

Dear Ones:

I so appreciate all of you who are reading and sometimes responding to this. It's great therapy for me to write it, and I hope that once in a while, it makes you laugh or otherwise resonates for you.

Yesterday I had my final "planning session" prior to radiation. I dutifully changed into the blue cotton robe I had been issued for the duration and waited my turn in the coed "Gowned Radiation Waiting" room (I love that "gowned" modifies "radiation") until I was called—20 minutes late. (Turns out they have more patients than they can see in the allotted hours of the day, and I am double-booked with another woman—a *wee* bit disconcerting. But my picture is on my file folder, so I trust they won't mix us up!)

I was quickly introduced to four radiation techs who will be my daily companions for the next six and a half weeks and to "The Beamer"—my moniker for the machine that will deliver my radiation treatments. I lay on the table while they fussed over me, getting my body into exactly the right position—arms overhead in metal braces, a bolster here and there—and lined up thin green ribbons of laser-type lights projected by The Beamer with the Sharpie pen marks drawn on my chest last week. (This reminded me of something we did with graph paper and acetate in junior high geometry class, but damned if I can remember exactly what.) Then, using a little punching device that reminded me of a nail gun, one of the techs tattooed teeny dots at strategic points. "A few of these might sting," she said mildly, milliseconds before I screamed, "SHIT!" after she punched one particularly tender spot. Worst of all was the one right at the edge of my nipple. Few spots on our bodies are as sensitive as that one!

Afterward, I asked a few questions, including whether there was any medical reason for me to wear the standard-issue blue robe. "No," said one of the guys. "You can wear whatever you want." I felt a need to explain. "Well, you know, tattoos and uniforms are a bit reminiscent of Auschwitz." "You're OK as long as we don't offer you a shower," another quipped. But I hadn't been joking, nor did I find his response funny. The idea of my body being permanently marked really bothered me. And it bothered me that no one even asked how I might feel about it.

Today, I was back for my first treatment. Three of the regular techs were in the room, plus some other young man no one bothered to introduce. So I asked, "And who are *you*?" to which he replied, "Oh, sorry, I'm Ben." One of the techs explained, "He's thinking about going into this field." I said, as neutrally as possible, "It's probably a good idea to let the patient know who the people are in the room," meanwhile wondering, "What the hell does *that* mean? Is this somebody's nephew who's thinking maybe radiation technology will make a good career? Or did he just come to the door this morning and say, 'Gee, can I watch?' " Honestly, I'm not very modest, but getting naked with strangers in Medical World over and over again doesn't get easier. I felt no less vulnerable today than I did the first time I had a needle biopsy, in 2008. (That day six or eight people were in the room, and the procedure I'd been told would take 30 minutes lasted an hour and a half. Turned out I was the guinea pig on a new machine, and some of those people weren't medical personnel but employees of the company that manufactures the machine. And no, they didn't ask my permission in advance.)

I took a deep breath and just let it go. The whole process lasted less than 15 minutes; the radiation comprised only a few of those minutes. When I asked how many minutes the radiation actually lasted, the tech said it varies. The machine is programmed by dose, but there can be variations in how long it takes to deliver the dose. *Wow.* I'm trusting technology less and less these days.

When I left the room, one of the techs asked me to stop and be weighed. Although this was only my first treatment, each week on Thursday I will see the radiation oncologist, Dr. Gold, necessitating the taking of vitals. I hate being weighed, because I've found paying too much attention to my weight is unhealthy. Better to focus on eating well, exercising and so on than poundage. When I am asked to be weighed, I usually take off my shoes and my belt, if I have one on, so the comparison will be reasonable with whatever I am wearing next time. So I said to the tech in my Jovial Hollis voice, "Well, I'm just going to take off my belt and shoes — " and she barked, "I don't have time for that!" So I meekly got onto the scale and said, "Well, don't tell me what it says, then."

Then I was led down a hall to another room to wait for Dr. Gold, who was considerate and conversational as always and answered my few questions. I was in and out of the place in less than an hour.

But the whole process was actually much creepier than I had anticipated. I had convinced myself that it would be no big deal, because I knew you can't feel the radiation and I would not likely have any side effects for several weeks, as I've been told they're cumulative. But, in fact, it did feel like a big deal. It felt *dehumanizing*. What has happened to our healers that they have lost touch with the fact that patients are people? There were three techs in the room when I was being tattooed by a fourth. How come one of them didn't say, "Hey, I'm going to hold your hand, and you just give me a good squeeze if it hurts." And how many seconds would have been lost if the tech had allowed me to take off my belt and shoes before being weighed? As a chaplain, I have seen many patients do odd things and make strange requests. Why not indulge them/us? Sick and dying people often have almost no control of their lives; shouldn't we let them demand Coke instead of Pepsi or refuse to have their blood taken for the fourth time today? One of my most balanced patients brought her own pajamas and robes every time she was hospitalized, and her husband decorated her entire room with stuffed animals and flowers. She refused to let go of her identity; she wasn't just a patient but an individual person. I am convinced this has helped her survive a serious chronic illness.

So, tomorrow I am wearing my leopard-spotted fleece robe to treatment. Next Thursday, if Miss "I'm too busy" is the weigh-in master, I'm not stepping on the scale. And if Ben or any other unidentified folks show up when I'm naked, I'm asking them to leave or take off *their* clothes — their choice.

Love,
Hollis

Cancer Journal

February 22

I had my first radiation yesterday, and this morning I feel depressed, resentful and unhappy. The Wednesday planning session, where I went into the radiation room for the first time and was tattooed and had to (once again) bare my breast in front of strangers without the slightest acknowledgment that it's a difficult thing to do, added insult to injury. And the tattoos hurt like hell, and that wasn't acknowledged, either. They should be more forthcoming about the pain. They should offer pain-reduction techniques: deep breathing, other imagery.

Then yesterday the same technician (who did the tattoo) was rude to me—wouldn't let me take off my belt and shoes to be weighed. I felt like a kid controlled by authority figures, as if it were a replay of my childhood medical experience, in which I had no choices. I see now that I truly do have PTSD from my childhood experiences (though I do not believe I am overreacting or that my assessments of disrespect in the clinical setting are therefore not accurate). But during my childhood experiences in Medical World, though my mother was loving and nurturing—pretty much the perfect mom for a sick kid—she could not have known how deeply it was affecting me or that she should have demanded to go into the exam room with me every time, for example. Even now, no one but I understands how that felt, and I have been trying to grapple with it sideways for a long time.

This is a "second descent" for me, as John Tarrant would put it.[7] I did the surgery and survived and this is the second "test" I must pass, this radiation. Because of my personal past, it feels like

---

7 The fabulous book this comes from is Tarrant's *The Light Inside the Dark: Zen, Soul, and the Spiritual Life* (1998, HarperCollins Publishers).

torture. But I also know my experience is not unique. Other women I've talked to about this process have found it equally disturbing.

Today I realize that the incident with the young male student yesterday was an eerie replay of my first sigmoidoscopy as a child, when, without my permission or even notification, the doctor performing the exam on my 10-year-old body invited a group of young male interns into the room to watch—while I lay butt up on the exam table as he stuck a stainless steel tube up my anus. No wonder I got triggered yesterday.

But I am not 10 years old now. I am going to take back the power that was taken from me as a child, and is being taken from me now, and exercise it to protect me.

Cancer Journal

February 24

Illness has forced me to look at my body—really look at it—in ways I have not before. It has been, in a way, just a house for my mind and soul. Now that I understand clearly that the continuation of me on this earthly plane depends entirely on this "house," I see it in a different way. I notice things about it I never noticed. Since the surgery, and now, during radiation, my breast has changed. All the swelling is gone, but the surface of the skin has remained pinker than my other breast (and may get pinker still as radiation goes on). My left nipple is not as reactive as my right (somehow desensitized by nerve damage?), so that if I am cold and my right nipple goes into "gooseflesh" mode, my left doesn't. Only now—seven weeks post-surgery—have I closely examined the scar under my breast to feel a little skin tag or rough place at one end; I will ask the doc if it should be removed, or maybe it will go away on its own. Perhaps after the trauma of radiation....

But overall, I am having more of a relationship with my body than in the past. It may be that I have been dissociated in some ways from my body since I was a child and was ill for so long. Dissociating was the only way I had to cope with the pain and the mistreatment I suffered in Medical World. Now it's time to reinhabit me! Get out of my head and into my body. Hopefully, doing some bodywork—getting some massage and acupuncture and doing yoga—will help.

Numinous moments: I had received a call from a young woman who's a native of Santa Fe. She lives in Berkeley, and she and her husband plan to be married here June 29. I'd had one conversation on the phone with her and agreed to officiate at the wedding. Then I was at the cancer center when the nurse who took my vitals mentioned, upon seeing the ankh I was wearing (I decided to wear it every day to radiation, since the ankh symbolizes life force), said,

"My daughter wears an ankh." Then he mentioned he'd noticed I was a minister on my file. He asked if I do weddings and funerals, and I said yes.

Later, as I was waiting, he came to find me and told me his daughter was the one I was going to marry! He felt like a warm and generous person, and we connected right away. What synchronicity. Then later, as I was leaving, he approached again, concerned about my privacy. If he told his daughter he had met me, then she would know—since he works at the cancer center—that I was likely a patient with cancer. He was genuinely worried: What to do? "Oh, that's OK," I told him. "I'm of the mind that we all need to talk about these things, to normalize them." It's true; it's part of why I'm writing the Booby Blog. We need to get cancer and all medical problems out of the closet, get rid of the stigma attached to disease. We are all going to be sick at one time or another, after all.

My friend Candy and I finally had breakfast this week. We talked of the arc of our illnesses and treatments. She has just come out of near isolation from a life-threatening chronic disease. She talked of how she has spent hours on the phone with insurers, medical and social service agencies and others, patiently asking questions, call after call, day after day, just to get the information she needed about her illness and how to get care. I told her how, the day after my diagnosis, I went to the office supply and bought a fat, pink, five-subject, spiral-bound notebook and a shimmery blue plastic expanding file and started saving every scrap of paper, receipt, report, referral—everything related to my care. I've taped the business card of every nurse, doctor, social worker, laboratory, etc. into it. I've written down the name of every person I encountered. In short, I have applied all of my old reporter skills to this work as if it were my job—and we agreed, it is a full-time job to be sick. Luckily, Candy qualified for Medicare two months before her diagnosis and she also has some insurance, just as I was blessed by Medicaid. We had, as we always seem to have, a wonderful, deep conversation.

I had asked the hypnotherapist Lori to make me a recording to listen to through my radiation treatment. I had written part of a script and given it to her, and she indicated she might use it. It irked me that she didn't seem receptive to my script and I later realized it is because I am so convinced that I need to be the author of my own healing. I need to hear my own words, my own beliefs about my recovery, more than anyone else's. No one else is doing this for me. I am Chiron, in his cave, learning to heal myself and, with any luck, will come out able to heal others through my work as well.[8]

---

8 Chiron is the centaur of Greek mythology—the father of medicine.

Cancer Journal

February 25

Full moon Tuesday. Awoke tired and for the past few days have tried to take afternoon naps. Could this be the fatigue that radiation can cause, or am I simply more attuned to my body now? Perhaps I simply didn't get enough protein yesterday? I have been craving protein since the surgery—mostly red meat cravings, which came on really strong a few weeks after surgery (and which I have been indulging: organic, grass-fed beef, bison, yak burgers).

Perhaps this is like most of my experience with Medical World: They tell you how you might feel, the aftereffects of surgery or the "proven" side effects of radiation or a drug, but they don't focus on them and seem, in fact, to minimize them. The pain and discomfort of the lumpectomy were minimized, I felt. When I asked my surgeon what to expect, she said, "Everyone is different." Not very helpful, that! I felt blindsided by the pain and particularly the length of time I was in notable discomfort (the kind you can't ignore), and it affected my ability to live my life.

Whereas, if she'd been a bit more specific ("You're a runner? There's a good chance you will feel too tender to run for a month, or maybe two."), it would have been helpful.

So now, feeling tired makes me feel a bit crazy: Is this all in my head? What does that mean, anyway? It's that contemporary Western cultural notion that body and mind can be parsed, that any illness can be categorized as "mental" versus "physical." At this point in my life, I do not believe that at all. What's shocking is that Western allopathic medicine remains so rooted in the corpus. The only physician I have seen so far who has said anything about lifestyle or the recent events of my life and their effects has been Dr. Heller, the "alternative" doc. Unbelievable.

Cancer Journal

February 27

Jennifer thinks my fatigue could be caused by allergies, as the spring winds are now up and the juniper is no doubt spreading its golden pollen haze over everything. (I have had to try hard not to take those statements as her challenging my experience or diminishing it.) So I went online again to look up radiation side effects and for the first time ended up on a site called breastcancer.org. There I found a whole list of side effects that my own doctors had not mentioned to me!

I'd been told about the "sunburning" effects of radiation on the skin, and fatigue and that both were cumulative—that is, I was more likely to feel them as time went on than immediately. The other side effects included armpit discomfort (pain, swelling, numbness due to nerve damage from surgery, exacerbated by skin irritation caused by the sunburn effect); chest pain (irritated nerves, similarly); heart problems; lowered white blood cell counts, which create a higher risk of infection; and lung problems. Good to know. Maybe the totality of these effects is why one sees the doctor every week during treatment. Or maybe that's simply to justify billing to insurance. Or both.

I am reminded that after surgery my hair seemed to be falling out more than usual; my hairbrush was full of it. I thought perhaps it was a side effect of anesthesia. I asked my surgeon about it and she said general anesthesia doesn't have that effect; it was probably due to stress. I could buy that, but something about it niggled at me. "Stress" always seems to be a convenient answer to patients' questions about issues that lack black-and-white, statistically proven answers. Back to the computer I went. And there it was, in a peer-reviewed medical journal article, a clinical study that said general anesthesia for surgery can cause hair loss. So there!

Cancer Journal

March 1

It is fascinating how this illness has drawn particular people into my life. After my diagnosis, friends began to recommend that I call so-and-so, their longtime friend who had had breast cancer. "I'll call her and tell her to expect your call," they'd offer. Some of these friends of friends I'd met once at a dinner party. Others were strangers. I dutifully took down numbers but wondered, what am I going to do? Call up and say, "Hi, I'm Hollis. Tell me about your breast cancer"? So although I followed up on a list of the referrals and threads others presented to me, I didn't place many of those calls.

And yet, a friend of mine here in Santa Fe with whom I had not been in contact since my return last April heard through the grapevine of my diagnosis. Though she had had breast cancer two times, she didn't call me. But she did pass along my contact information to a mutual friend of ours who had long ago moved to California and now has breast cancer as well. Janet called and we had a long talk. She is in the health-care field, in the alternative end, and she is aggressively advocating for herself and refusing most treatments offered. It was a good "consultation" to hear a trusted longtime friend echo the suspicions and fears I have about the system and its cookie-cutter approach to care. Not to mention how lovely it was just to reconnect.[9]

---

9 This same friend later emailed and asked me to remove her from the Booby Blog email list. She did not believe in the treatments I was pursuing, and it bothered her to read about them, she later told me. I have come to understand that for some of us to believe in our own path, we must see it as the singular *right* path. I prefer to believe that each of us must find our own paths to healing, and they can be and often are startlingly different.

One friend of a friend I did eventually call was Janine. Janine had been told, when first diagnosed, that her cancer was of such an aggressive type that she likely would die within three months. I had not met Janine when I called her, but our mutual friend talked of her so often that I felt I knew her. I knew, for example, that her husband had died within the last year. So I called, and Janine told me the story of her two mastectomies and her recovery, including the miraculous IV infusions of "biological medicine" that had healed her. Sometime later, we met and talked further. At one point, after having explained to me what a marvelous job her surgeon had done on both her mastectomies, she said, "Do you want to see my scars?" She lifted up her top to reveal two thin, perfect, horizontal scars across her chest. She did not look butchered or disfigured at all! Despite missing nipples or any vestige of breasts, she somehow looked normal, as if that were the way her chest was meant to be.

"I used to wear a fake set of double-D boobs that I could put in bras," she said, "but I gave that up because I just don't care." And, she noted, "Now, I could go outside with no shirt on! How could it be indecent exposure?" We laughed. "Do you want to see my scar?" I asked back, laughing internally at this grown-up version of the I'll-show-you-mine-if-you'll-show-me-yours" game we played as curious 6-year-olds. She admired my relatively tiny scars as I had admired her long ones. Eventually I had to leave to make it to my radiation appointment, but I felt I had been of service to her, and she to me. It was one of those out-of-space, out-of-time experiences that I would not forget.

I wonder about our discussion of her being able to reveal her chest without violating any sort of exposure law. "What are they gonna do?" she had said, sounding a bit like a rebellious child. Even though exposure laws are inherently sexist and reflect our society's prudish ideas about the human body, that position also rejects femininity in a way: Since no breasts are there, there is nothing to hide; without those emblems of femaleness, there is nothing to cherish and hold close, protect, reserve for one's self and one's lover. That seems very oddly anti-feminist. Yet when I saw Janine's beautiful scars and flat chest, which revealed her bone structure and musculature in a way we cannot see on a woman with breasts,

I immediately thought of the Amazon women of Greek mythology, who were said to have cut off their right breasts so that they could better draw a bow to shoot an arrow (no mention of left-handed Amazons, curiously). I saw in Janine a warrior woman, a survivor; how strong she had to be, to go through two mastectomies and to come back, through seeking her own healing, from a three-month death sentence. What an amazing woman. (Amazing=Amazonian: Although the root of the two words is not, according to etymologists, the same, I like to pretend it is.)

Other people have sifted into my life. My friends Nancy and Betty offered up their friend Sandra, who had had breast cancer. ("Don't you remember meeting her at my birthday party five years ago?" Ummmmm. Kinda.) I took her number but didn't call. Then one day I was at the cancer center for an appointment and ran into a couple I had known for years. Both had cancer and were undergoing treatment. As we talked, a woman came over to greet them and she looked vaguely familiar. It was Sandra. We sat in the lobby and talked for an hour. Our chance meeting was truly a serendipitous event. She had been on a spiritual path for a few years, and I shared some of my story of attending seminary and pursuing clinical chaplaincy training. She shared her breast cancer story with me. Especially important was her advice that she had expected to feel "normal" the day after her radiation ended, but in fact it took a few more months before she felt herself back in the groove. No one had suggested such a thing to me; in fact it seems de rigueur not to offer all the facts up front but to dribble them out—and often only in response to specific questions.

I realize now that the failure to acknowledge suffering is a huge mistake on the part of our medical community. To acknowledge suffering must trigger in the clinician the desire to "fix," the obligation to do something—offer advice, a different drug, another idea. But in fact it is not the "fix" that is most important or needed. It's the acknowledgement, the hearing of another's pain, which lessens the suffering. Got a great new drug I could try? Wonderful. But could you put your hand on my shoulder and say, "I am sorry you are feeling so bad," "I see that your skin is so burned. How does it feel? Like itching, or stabbing, or hot? Tell me about it." We need to tell someone about it to release some of our suffering. We need to speak it out loud. I would love to do an in-service training about this. It's basic to chaplaincy training. Why don't doctors and nurses and techs get this? How different I would have felt if my radiation techs had said something besides a chirpy "Hi!" each time I walked in.

Booby Blog #14

March 1

Dear Ones:

Today was Day Seven of radiation treatment, and I've already adopted a routine for myself: I get up in the morning, do my spiritual practice (largely journaling and reading), eat breakfast, shower (following all the rules, such as no shaving left armpit, no deodorant, lotions or other products on skin) and walk out the door at 10:25 a.m. to make the 15-minute drive to the cancer center. Much is DIY from there: Sign in at the front desk, walk back to "Gowned Radiation Waiting," go into dressing room, take off upper body garments, put on robe, wait to be called, greet the four techs, hop on the table, pull my robe off my left arm, lie down, wait while they line up the laser lights with the tattoos on my chest and leave the room, watch while The Beamer makes its arc over the table and sends those invisible rays through my body, get dressed again and—voila!—I'm out of there, usually within 20 minutes.

I've added a few things to ritualize the event. I *am* wearing my leopard-spotted, black-and-white fuzzy short robe (with fuchsia satin piping and lining!) instead of the ugly blue standard-issue cotton robe (which, my radiation oncologist informs me, is a great improvement over the hospital gowns they used to give patients). While I'm in the dressing room, I anoint and bless myself with the same homemade eucalyptus oil I use on patients and ministry clients. Once I am on the table in the big, darkened radiation room, the arm of The Beamer, which terminates in a giant round disc, starts radiating me from my right side, then crosses above me in an arc to my left side, where it pauses and radiates me again. If I were the Nile River, it's as if the sun is tracing its daily path from east to west across me. (I know it is the Earth that moves around the sun, and not the other way around, but hey, the ancient Egyptians didn't.) During the 90 seconds or so of radiation, I invoke the Egyptian sun god, Ra, to dissolve and release all the cells I no longer need, to rejuvenate healthy cells and to stimulate the growth of new healthy cells. (I just can't buy into the battleground metaphor of "killing" off the "enemy"cells. These are my cells; they've just outlived their usefulness and gotten rather cranky!) It all probably sounds a little crazy, but it brings me peace of mind.

Every day after radiation, I take myself to do some other kind of treatment or activity that is healthy. I've hunted down high-quality, inexpensive places to get what I need: We the People Community Acupuncture Clinic (don't you love that?) charges a self-determined sliding scale of $15 to $40; the Community Yoga Center offers $5 classes at noon; a local spa offers far-infrared sauna (recommended by my alternative M.D. for detoxing), 10 sessions for $100. So even though I don't have a regular income, I am, with the help of a few generous friends, able to really focus on my healing and recovery. I'm also taking walks, though not yet running; that may have to wait until a few months after treatment ends.

If I sound like I'm doing well—well, I am. Even the tech who acted like Nurse Ratched on my first day has softened up a bit. I am experiencing some fatigue and skin discomfort, but so far, I can't complain. Thank you all for your support, good thoughts and prayers. *Those* beams I welcome without reservation.

And, as I told all my techs today when we bid each other farewell for the weekend, "Have fun first—then do the chores!"

Love,
Hollis

Cancer Journal

March 4

Another person from my past has floated back into my life as part
of this journey with breast cancer: Jacqui. She is a masseuse I
wrote an article about in 2008 who was "circuit-riding" at the time,
going to ranches spread out all over Northern New Mexico to treat
the sick and dying. I had not seen her since writing the article but
ran into her at a December meeting of Santa Fe Doorways, an
end-of-life organization. I told her I had breast cancer, recalling
that she had pursued a certificate in oncology massage. Indeed she
has spent the last two years working on that and offered to give
me treatments. But, given my financial condition, I didn't follow
through. I don't think it's pride that prevented me so much as the
feeling that we women are so seldom paid what we are worth that
I don't feel OK about asking another underpaid woman for a dis-
count.

So a month or two went by, and I did not communicate with
Jacqui. Then one day I received an email from her. She had a pain
in her breast—it had been going on for some time—and she was
having a cancer scare. We communicated for about 10 days—by
email, oddly. I think I was so busy with my own issues in the beginning of radiation that I could not make time to call. And then,
thankfully, her "scare" was over. Nothing showed up in a mammogram. Whatever it is, it is probably not dire, and she is following
up. Then she wrote to offer me free massage, explaining in more
detail her training. Now I will take her up on it, feeling we each
have something to offer the other and that I will actually benefit her
in a way by being another "practice subject." [10]

---

10 Sadly, Jacqui's pain later proved to be a symptom of lung cancer. I was
able to spend time with her at her home—as her friend and as a chaplain—
while she was on hospice care. She died July 23.

One more thing this morning before I race off to my many tasks: During a period of "midnight madness," the wee hours when I awaken and am unable to get back to sleep, it bubbled up in my consciousness that we are in Lent, and my final radiation planning session, the day I met The Beamer, was Ash Wednesday. That day, I assumed radiation would begin the next day and had done a rough calculation and determined my sessions would end on March 30. (I had not looked at a calendar or would have realized that day would have been a Saturday, when the center is closed.) The date also coincided with an appointment I had made eight months ago for a tattoo with a popular tattoo artist. Jennifer had given me a "down payment" for a tattoo as a birthday present long before my diagnosis. But once I had the diagnosis, I had envisioned the tattoo as the Egyptian goddess Isis, in her classic pose with wings outspread, over my left breast (which at that point I envisioned missing entirely). None of these has quite materialized—I still have all but a golf ball-sized hunk of my left breast; radiation did not start the day after the last planning session but a week later, changing my projected completion date to April 9; and I have since learned that I cannot have a tattoo for a few months after radiation, as it is likely my skin will still be sunburned and sore.

Nevertheless, my radiation treatment is occurring roughly during the period of Lent. The Greek and Hebrew words for "temptation" also mean (or more precisely mean) "test" or "trial." While I don't feel I am being tempted (in the usual meaning of the word), I certainly feel tested, or challenged. This is an initiation. I will be reborn, somehow, when I come out of this wilderness. I am finding so much of interest on this spiritual journey.

Booby Blog #15

March 13

Dear Ones:

Today was Day 13 of 34 radiation treatments. Last week I missed two treatments when the radiation machine was on the blink, so my end date is now something like April 11. This week I shifted to a 7:45 a.m. appointment, and because I am the first patient of the day, there's no waiting! The cancer center has gotten so busy in the last few weeks that it has been perpetually behind. (What's up with that? "Wow! It's spring, I think I'll get radiation!") I have to leave the house at 7:25, so it's almost like having a regular day job.

I had a breakthrough in self-care last week when, for the second time, a strange person was in the radiation treatment room and no one bothered to introduce me. I'm not a stickler for manners, but hey, I'm taking my clothes off here. Don't I deserve to know who's watching? Like last time, it was a young man who turned out to be a radiation student. "C'mon guys," I said to the regular techs. "You know the deal with me." I turned to the student. "OK, who are you?" I asked. "Oh, I'm Joe"—he shuffled nervously—"and I'm a student, and I hope it's OK that I observe." I'm sure I let loose a long-suffering sigh, but I said OK.

While I lay on the table and The Beamer made its radiating arc over me, I decided it really wasn't OK. I feel strongly that patients should be asked permission before anyone comes in who isn't a licensed medical staff member who *has* to be in the room. And even if I gave a global OK for student observers, I would expect the student of the day to be introduced to me. Furthermore, shouldn't the student be practicing proper patient communication skills anyway? (Although the licensed folk certainly aren't modeling that behavior!) I decided I'd done my part for the future of radiation technology: No more students for me.

When I left the room, I marched straight into Dr. Gold's office (fuzzy leopard-print bathrobe and all, having forgotten, in my nervousness and pique, to change first) and asked him politely to put a note on my chart that I did not want students in my treatments anymore. For a brief second, he hesitated, and I felt sure he was going to either ask why or try to dissuade me, but I suspect he saw the look in my eye, and responded, "No problem." (This guy's a really decent man, one of the "good guys.") It was then I turned and began to walk out of the clinic—before realizing I hadn't changed clothes. I tried to act nonchalant as I sneaked back into the dressing room.

Yay, me—I stood up for myself! Later I doubted my behavior and felt foolish, but as a friend pointed out, I really didn't have to fear any consequences. The techs weren't going to turn The Beamer on "high" just because I didn't want students in the room, and did I really care if they didn't like me or started calling me Cat Woman?

Since then, everyone has behaved normally (all the students I've spotted are lurking *outside* the radiation room), and I am working feverishly (in my mind) on the training I'm going to develop and present on patient sensitivity for medical personnel and sell to hospital and health-care corporations for large sums of money.

All things considered, my sense of humor is intact, and my many friends keep laughing at my jokes, so I'm happy. Jennifer is in China for three weeks, so I miss her. But Karen, my BFF of nearly 30 years, came and spent five days with me and treated me like a princess (including a luxurious spa day), which was grand.

Happy spring, and thanks for listening!

Love,
Hollis

Booby Blog #16

March 16

Dear Ones:

Today, for the first time since November—when they began sticking needles in my breast—I decided I would go for a run. I went over to Frenchy's Field and picked up the Santa Fe River Trail (a.k.a. the Santa Fe Dry Arroyo Trail). I ran (OK, honestly? I run/walk ... with *lots* of walking) east on the paved trail along the riverbed, crossed a little pedestrian bridge and started back west on a dirt path. It felt good to finally be running again. I had begun last June and worked up to running 2 1/2 miles five or six days a week along the Santa Fe River on the east side of town where I was then living. Today I had a little trepidation about falling—it was an unfamiliar path—but I had also worried a bit about falling when I was running last year. I dismissed the thought today, as I had then.

So you've already guessed that I fell. Rather spectacularly. A total face plant in the dirt. I felt myself going, as we always do, and tried to somehow catch myself, but down I went, hitting hardest on my hands and face. I got up right away and then decided perhaps I should sit down for a moment. Nothing seemed broken. My face felt numb, but no blood was spurting out anywhere. I had to spit out grit, but my tongue counted all teeth intact. So I just had a short but good cry. I felt incredibly vulnerable and alone sitting there in the dirt.

I instantly realized this was the third time in about three days that I had done something in a moment of unconsciousness that caused me grief: I'd gotten stopped by a cop near my house doing 40 in a 25-mile-per-hour zone (and got a $116 ticket); I'd taken off my watch and misplaced or lost it; and now I'd managed to take my eyes off the trail long enough to trip and fall. Perhaps I am not quite yet myself, I thought, and should have waited a bit longer to start running again. Maybe radiation causes "brain fog," as does chemotherapy.

Soon I got up, dusted myself off and made my way back to the car. I ran some of the way—on the paved path, that is. Once home, I shifted into self-care mode. Maybe I needed a day off from obligations. Maybe I should just ditch the "to-do" list for the day. Maybe I should sit on the sofa and read a book. I started by drawing a hot bath with lavender Epsom salts while I doctored my face and hands. I noticed that my scrapes matched up with old childhood wounds: The road burns under my chin were adjacent to the scar I'd earned at age 3 when my sister pushed me down the slide (she swears she didn't push me, but that's *her* story); and I'd landed in the dirt on my right cheek, the cheek that broke the windshield when I was in an auto accident at 15.

Much of my experience in Medical World these days reminds me of those childhood experiences and others. I also had a chronic intestinal disease as a child. All told, I spent much more time than the average kid in doctors' offices and the hospital. I see this current experience as an interesting echo of that era, only this time around I have agency to make my own decisions about my treatment, whereas then I had none. I get to sift through the recommendations made to me and decide which I want to take and which I want to decline and to seek out others that might work for me.

As time has gone on, I've felt more and more strongly that I must be what I call "the author of my own healing," realizing in the process that being the author (the "author-ity") of one's own healing also means taking responsibility for it. Our current Western medical paradigm asks that patients give up control to their physicians and the system. For people who don't have the wherewithal to make their own decisions, that works. But it also works if they aren't cured or don't get well; then they can blame the docs and the institution (along with God). I'm speaking from experience here, having heard patients and/or their family members blaming the progression of a disease on their health-care providers.

I'm making my own decisions and taking responsibility for myself, and sometimes that's scary. I don't mean to suggest that doing so is necessarily heroic; it may just be a matter of wanting to be in control. When I told an acquaintance with breast cancer who happens to be nurse and runs cancer support groups that I likely wouldn't take the estrogen-blocking drugs that are recommended to women like me post-radiation, she said, "Well, now, you're going to want to think about how you'll feel if the cancer comes back." Like what? I was a bad, bad girl, and now I'm getting punished? *There are no guarantees.* I could do everything the establishment offers me and still have a recurrence. I could do everything I've found that may be helpful and still have a recurrence. I could do nothing at all, and the cancer might never come back! I think I prefer to use my brain and my intuition and take my chances rather than buy into the party line without questioning it. No one and nothing will be to blame if my cancer recurs. We simply don't know enough about cancer yet to be able to say much at all about it with certainty.

Speaking of intuition, I clearly wasn't listening this morning when that little voice in my head warned me about falling. Some part of me knew I wasn't really paying adequate attention! But I had a second chance today to listen to the little voice. After I treated my cuts and scrapes, I got into my big, hot bathtub (probably not advisable for the irradiated booby, but it felt darned good) and just sat for a while. When I finally got out, I felt dizzy, and the little voice said, "Sit down, Hollis." I ignored it, thinking this was a typical hot-water-standing-up-dizziness, but then it said again, "Really. Sit down!" So I plopped down onto the bathroom rug with my big, fluffy towel around me. I saw a few stars, as they say, little disappearing white dots dancing across my visual horizon. I'd fallen pretty hard, after all. Nina, the 9-month-old Chihuahua-corgi mix, decided my toweled lap was the perfect place for a snuggle and proceeded to lick Epsom-salty water off my neck. I let her.

While I sat there, I was struck again by that feeling of utter vulnerability. What did I *want*? I asked myself. What would assuage that terrible ache? Mommy, of course; I'm hurt and I want my mommy! No matter that I am 56 years old. Surely everyone wants Mommy (a good mommy, if theirs wasn't the perfect nurturer like mine) when they are hurt, no matter what their age. In fact, I'd been a pretty good mommy to myself so far: I'd fixed up my boo-boos, had a hot bath and was going to have a nice lunch and take the rest of the day off from responsibility. The only thing missing was someone to tuck me into bed and say, "There, there, it won't hurt for long. You'll be just fine tomorrow." And honestly, Nina was doing a good job of mimicking that voice, her little pink tongue lapping earnestly at my neck. (Who knew dogs had a proclivity for Epsom salts?) We sat in companionable silence for a bit before I determined it was safe to get up and make some comfort food—scrambled eggs—for lunch. I managed to muster the energy for a trip to the post office and Trader Joe's before coming home for a two-hour nap. I ran into my friend Robin at Trader Joe's, and she ended our five-minute chat by commenting on how good I looked. "Really?" I said, dubious. "I fell on my run this morning, and I'm all scraped up." She peered at me and shrugged. "I didn't notice." Later in the day, another friend I spoke to on the phone said she'd passed me in the car on my way to the store. "You looked really pretty today," she said.

Scabby, puffy and still looking good, even pretty? Honestly? Well, theologically, at least, it works. We are all broken, as my friend and fellow minister Penny often reminds me. *And* we are also perfect, just as we are. Despite this day's reminder that I am now—and always—a vulnerable human being, somehow I came across to my friends just fine, even pretty.

Now *that's* good medicine, eh?

Much love and good health to you all,

Hollis

Cancer Journal

March 20

Yesterday was my 17th radiation session — exactly halfway through. I am very tired these days, a few hours after radiation, just as they predicted. I am taking naps. Most days I allow myself an hour, but if I have the luxury of not setting an alarm, I sleep for two. But I ask myself, how do I know this is the radiation? A few weeks ago we made the switch to Daylight Saving Time — "spring forward" — and that is always cause for sleepiness. Also, as Jennifer noted, it's allergy season, although I seem to have few symptoms. A teeny bit of a runny nose, but nothing like I've had in the past. I wonder, if my immune system is depressed by radiation, does it make sense that I would have lessened allergies, since allergies are an immune response? Could this be a sort of hidden benefit of radiation? It's an interesting idea, anyway. Jennifer thinks it's because I'm on her gluten-free diet. The body is such a mystery. It's all a crapshoot, as Dad used to say.

Last night I was getting ready for bed when a little feeling sneaked up and pinched me. It felt like the tattoo machine, in my chest: "When do I get to go back to my normal life?" It was nostalgia for the innocence of immortality, maybe, or youth — in the sense that the body seems indestructible. I am now vulnerable. There is a big crack under the door, and the wind is blowing in, and there is nothing to be done about it. It disappeared — the clarity of that feeling — almost as soon as I recognized it, like a mouse that had sneaked under that crack into the room, saw me and fled terrified back into the hallway. This is why the Tibetan Buddhists practice contemplation of death: to stare the mouse in the face, invite it in, give it a lap and some cheese, discover the nature of mouse-ness. And because it is there in the walls all the time, in any case; just because we don't see it doesn't mean it's not there.

In a similar vein of confronting the truth about my illness and the nature of mortality, I have realized a few times with stunning clarity that despite my best rational intentions I am still, on and off, indulging in magical thinking. My magical thoughts go like this: If I follow all the treatment protocols I have set up for myself, after doing research and with good intentions, the cancer will go away and won't come back. If I do enough of the yoga, acupuncture, infrared saunas, electromagnetic pulse therapy, running, supplements, radiation, I will be OK. If not, however, if I "cheat" and do not continue to do all these things enough or correctly, then the cancer will likely come back.

My über-rational mind recognizes this as faulty thinking. Yes, it is entirely possible that all I am doing will support my overall healing. And that the spiritual work I am doing—examining and clearing up issues rooted in my past, reconciling old relationships, etc.—also may help mitigate the return of this illness to my body.

But that's all. No guarantees, as I wrote in the Booby Blog. Still, I want to wrest value from my personal suffering so that it has meaning. I am in the Viktor Frankl club rather than the Susan Sontag club on this issue.[11] The alternative seems to be nihilism. Oh, sometimes I wish I had a better background in philosophy, so I had clearer language and thinking on these issues instead of a CliffsNotes level of understanding. But surely I get points for asking the questions, however poorly articulated?

On a related note, just as my immortality sneaked up and bit me last night, so, too, do I occasionally have a sudden realization that for a time I have forgotten that I have cancer. I have been thinking/feeling/acting without any awareness that I am ill or any different from other people I come into contact with. Then I feel guilty, like the bereaved person when she forgets her spouse has died: How could she? I have recognized this and so many aspects of my psycho-spiritual response to this illness as parallels to the

---

11 Frankl wrote *Man's Search for Meaning*, about how finding meaning was essential to those who survived the Nazi concentration camps, himself included. Sontag's *Illness as Metaphor* challenged attitudes that blame the victim for her illness, but in doing so, she negated finding meaning in illness.

grief response. I mustn't forget my invisible companion or...what? It will come back with a vengeance? I will be punished? Yes, I think that's the unconscious thought. Complicated responses.

And I have wondered many times, should I say, "I have breast cancer" or "I had breast cancer"? No way to know which is rationally true. There may be cancer cells still in my breast. They say cancer cells—that is, mutated, abnormal cells—are always in our bodies, but our bodies normally dispatch them. It's when our bodies can't get rid of them and they proliferate that we develop tumors or "chronic" cancers like leukemia. Still—no tumor, no cancer? I "had" it? I have compromised so far—in the past month or so— by saying, "I was diagnosed with..." or "Since I was diagnosed...," thereby avoiding the question of the present or past tense of "to have." (Perhaps only someone obsessed with language asks such questions.)

Beyond rationality is the notion that by saying, "I had breast cancer," I am affirming its eradication from my body. I'm not in denial that I had it, or that it could still threaten me, but I am claiming my healing, focusing on the positive. I don't really see a downside to that, although it might sound odd to some people. Unless I am remiss to give up my new "special status" as Hollis-With-Breast-Cancer? Is that playing the victim role? Is there a certain part of me, however small and closeted, that has enjoyed the drama of it all? I think if I am honest I have to say yes. One gets a lot of attention, mostly positive, from illness, and I know as a child that though my illness was painful, physically and emotionally, I also got an enormous amount of attention, especially from my mother, because of it. (In contrast, one friend of mine who is never sick and refuses to even acknowledge when she has a cold informed me that her mother of eight was too busy to pay any attention to a sick child; her theory was she didn't get sick as an adult because she learned as a child she wouldn't gain anything by it.) Now I am getting kindness from others, chiefly people who care about me, and in that sense it has been deeply supportive. It has also afforded me the opportunity to accept my own need for love and attention and to not feel ashamed or less than stoic for doing so.

But as I write this, I realize that the person from whom I have reaped the most loving attention, most deservedly, and which has been the most healing is me! This cancer has signaled me that I am deserving of my own loving care. And I have been giving it to myself. If I "get well"—when I decide I am "healed" (at least for now)—do I have to stop focusing on and loving myself? I think that is the crux of the question. I must find a way to answer no, to say, I must continue to keep the focus on me in order to stay healed, or at least try. Looking inward, doing my own personal work, is the key not only to my healing but also to my ability to serve others. Only if my own heart is clear and open can I be of much good to anyone else.

Certainly my life will shift when radiation and any aftereffects are over, and certainly I will have to find better ways to support myself financially, but the self-focus is a good thing for the long term.

Cancer Journal

March 24

Back to the Q&A session I had with Dr. Gold, the radiation on-cologist, on Friday: I put my left-brained rational reporter hat on and peppered him with questions, all of which he was able to an-swer, and, thankfully, he never seemed defensive or insulted. I got a lot more clarity about the radiation and therefore felt more able to comply with the protocol. I had to sort of tell myself, "For once, Hollis, quit fighting it and follow the rules. Stay with the process all the way through. See what happens if you 'belong' and act like it."

I think I will pray and ask my higher power to let me know un-equivocally if I should stop radiation early. Otherwise, I will do the protocol, recognizing my own propensity for thwarting the process (any process!). Oddly, when you complete your radiation at the cancer center, you are said to "graduate," and you get a certificate signed by your radiation oncologist and your techs. But any way you look at it, this is a solitary schooling; there is no class, and if there were, it would be one in which a lot of alumni wouldn't make it to the reunion.

Booby Blog #11

March 24

Dear Ones,

Update on the "face plant" event of last week: The scabs on the little scratches and road rash on my cheek and chin have disappeared, and except for a few lovely bruises elsewhere on my body, I am fine. However, I went to the dentist a few days after my fall for an annual checkup and he said, "Did you know your left front tooth is cracked stem to stern?" (OK, he didn't say "stem to stern." He said, "from top to bottom," but I've always liked the jaunty sound of the nautical phrase.) I explained my fall on the trail run. There's nothing to do about the crack, he said, except to avoid further "traumas," which could cause the tooth to break in half. "Do you—er—fall often when you're running?" he asked politely. (Was it my imagination, or did he glance at my silver hair when he asked that?)

I generally make it a habit to avoid traumas, but I am also considering calling one of those windshield repair places; if they can inject sealant into a windshield crack and guarantee it for the life of the car, why couldn't they do the same for my tooth? In fact, why hasn't the dental industry come up with a similar sealant? I'm calling my friend Brenda, who makes teeth (literally, she has her own lab and makes teeth for dentists) and telling her about my fabulous idea. She can develop a new product, experiment on my front tooth, make millions and give me a small kickback—say, $5 million and a bit of stock.

Radiation progress report: I am slightly more than halfway through the 34 treatments for which I am scheduled. So far, my worst side effect has been the nonnegotiable fatigue factor: Three or four hours after a treatment, I *have* to lie down for a nap of an hour or more. This is typical, I've been told, and because the radiation is cumulative, it comes on slowly, and it will possibly get worse as my treatment goes on. (Longer naps? Two naps a day?) I'm also showing signs of the "sunburn" the radiation causes on the skin; there's a perfect rectangle encompassing my left armpit and breast that is turning reddish-brown, as if I'd forgotten to put sunscreen on that one large area before taking a nude sunbath or I'd been a test subject for an early 1960s tanning lotion. (Remember QT, anyone? That orange-streaked skin?) I am dutifully smearing aloe vera gel on the burn and hoping it doesn't get much worse. Right now it's just mildly uncomfortable.

Nevertheless, I don't think I'll be taking advantage of my March 30 appointment for a tattoo (a birthday gift last year from Jennifer; this particular tattoo artist is booked eight months in advance)! Before I developed the beginning of the "sunburn," I had asked my radiation oncologist about the advisability of tattooing during treatments, and he said mildly it would be wise to wait until a few months after radiation is over, although he's had patients get tattoos *on* their surgery scars *while* they were getting radiation (without asking his advice, obviously). These people, I suspect, had access to a lot of Oxycodone.

It's spring, and we have daffodils on our dining room table. I hope you do, too. Thanks for listening!

Love,
Hollis

Cancer Journal

March 25

I realized this morning that I have set a false goal or deadline for myself. In my mind's eye I have somehow looked ahead and decided that, by June, all will be well. I think this originated when I had a conversation with Sandra, and she shared that she had thought that after her radiation ended she would wake up the next morning and somehow feel like herself, "normal" again. Instead it was a few months before she felt fully able to re-enter life. I have used that as a gauge for myself, knowing that sometime in June I will have my six-month follow-up mammogram, and it will be clear, and I will feel reborn and free to go on with my life.[12]

But I see now that is probably setting myself up for disappointment or a self-fulfilling prophecy. I may feel much like my "ordinary" self before then, or it could take longer. Or it may be that the "self" I once was, pre-cancer, is truly gone, dead, my "innocence" is truly lost and mortality has taken up residence in my spirit and psyche, in which case it really is a death-and-rebirth process I am undergoing. And since I am still in the middle of it, I cannot predict when I will come out, or how.

---

12 My follow-up mammogram actually didn't happen until August; it was supposed to be scheduled four months after the end of radiation.

Cancer Journal

March 26

I think of the people I meet in the "Gowned Radiation Waiting" room as the Cancer Club. The room is a like a 12-step meeting-house: Here are people from all walks of life one might never otherwise meet. We members of this strange club have different cancers, different stories, different skin colors and ethnicities and cultures and politics, but we all have cancer in common. Among the cast of characters in my time slots have been (1) an aging hippie male with thick, snow-white hair past his shoulders, contained by a neatly folded bandana around his forehead; (2) an 80-ish Hispanic man, tiny and frail, whose robe perpetually seemed poised to fall off and whose dementia led him to repeat himself daily, while waiting. "I was in the Army," he said, "and it was always 'Hurry up and wait.'" He said this over and over, every day; and (3) a perfectly coiffed, elegantly dressed 50-ish woman who never donned a gown, thus I suspected she was getting radiation to some part of her head, perhaps her brain.

Everyone in Northern New Mexico who needs radiation or full-on chemo has to come to this place; there is no other option except to go all the way to Albuquerque, an additional hourlong drive. Some people must drive two hours just to get to the cancer center here. Others make decisions about their treatment to minimize their trips here—because they cannot afford the time away from work, or the gas money, or have children or others they are responsible for on a daily basis. For example, a woman with a tumor like mine might get a mastectomy because then she would not need radiation and the daily trips it requires. It's shocking to think such serious decisions are made based on geography; that's something you never hear about on TV news magazines about cancer.

One of my first Cancer Club friends was a woman who drove three hours round-trip every day, in winter ice and snow, for her breast cancer radiation. She seemed a bit odd in our first conversation. She complained about her radiation sunburn, opening her gown to gaze at it curiously. I asked if she'd been given examples of the skin creams to use for the sunburn and she said no, complaining that "they" weren't doing enough for her, and how could she be expected to pay for that? I suggested she ask for some samples and wondered to myself why the staff had not offered her any as they had me. She did eventually get some samples, I learned later. While I was at the drugstore, examining the ingredients in a number of skin care products, I bought an extra tube for her. I put it in a pretty little gauze sack with a small card, wrote a blessing on it and gave it to her on her last treatment day. I am aware that I was acting like her "chaplain *du jour*," but I felt good about reaching out to her, and she appreciated it.

Booby Blog #10

April 1

Dear Ones:

Woohoo! I am on my way to the end of radiation treatments. Only three more "whole breast" treatments (why does it sound like I'm talking about buying chicken?) and then six "boosters," which brings to mind the childhood "booster shots" we got for measles and mumps and the like, doesn't it? The boosters target only the area where the tumor was removed on the theory that if any rogue cancer cells are floating around in there, they're probably partying down in the same general area as the original tumor. Dr. Gold keeps calling this area the "cavity," which sounds really creepy to me, like a dental cavity, or a gaping hole or something. From the outside, my boob just looks a bit smaller in that general area and, with the scar, well, a little pissed off, maybe. My nipple looks kind of like "Top o' the mornin' to ya!" these days because, in preparation for the boosters, they've marked me up with Sharpies again, and this time, right atop my nipple is a round circle with a dot in the middle and a line over it. Yep, sorta like the Egyptian "Eye of Horus." Which symbolized protection, good health and royalty. Bonus synchronicity: The Eye of Horus was also known as the Eye of Ra, and those of you with great reading retention skills will recall it's the Egyptian sun god, Ra, whom I invoke while The Beamer is "cooking" me each day. Each time I notice this new extra "eye" when I look in the mirror, I can't help but giggle just a little.

And, speaking of laughter as the best medicine, so many friends have asked, "How's the radiation going?" and then in the next breath they've said—with no sense of irony or realization of what they've articulated—"Well, you just look *radiant*," or, "You seem to be *glowing*." I am not making this up. While I am willing to believe I look pretty darned good these days, I find it hysterical that our unconscious minds deliver up the right words—literally!—for my situation.

On the somber side of things, I am so humbled every day while I sit among my fellow patients in the Gowned Radiation Waiting room. Sometimes I don't want to go in when they call my name, because I am having a conversation with another cancer patient, which seems so much more important. These days my early-morning companion is a man from out of town who arrives earlier than I do but whose appointment is after mine. We talk about the home he and his wife have in Mexico, how this year they couldn't go down there due to his diagnosis, how he hopes to fly down and pick up their RV so they can travel around stateside this summer. They missed the winter season down in Baja. I have no idea what kind of cancer he has or how serious his condition is. Like many of my older male patients when I was working as a chaplain in the hospital setting, he really needs to talk, but he prefers to keep it light and avoids mentioning his illness.

A woman who comes in a bit later carries a Kleenex box like a talisman, even though tissues are always available in the waiting room. She holds it tightly against her chest and has always remained remote. The other day we finally connected; she said she has throat cancer and her radiation protocol is supposed to be "the worst."

"I lost 10 pounds in the last week," she offered morosely. She coughs horribly, hence the tissues. That day when I left, she offered a little wave. Does she have a support system, a spouse or partner or sister who is walking with her through this, with whom she can talk? Or is she facing it all alone? It's impossible to know, and our encounters arc too brief to allow for lengthier conversations.

The other day my early-morning appointment was changed to midmorning because I had to have another "planning session" with a CT scan (for the boosters). When I parked my car and was gathering my things, I noticed a woman in the car next to me doing the same thing—only she was wrangling some flesh-colored, hard-plastic molded thing that I thought was perhaps a demonstration object, like fake breasts, for an educational workshop. What is that? I mused. I hopped out of my car and went in, soon forgetting about the puzzling object. While I was in the waiting room, a woman about my age came in with a towel wrapped around her waist. Now, most of us wear gowns (or in my case, my fabulous leopard-spotted fleece robe), so I couldn't help but wonder what she was doing with that towel. What if it fell off?

Without prelude, she spoke to me and the few other people in the room: "Do you have a raunchy sense of humor?" she asked. I nodded eagerly. Anything for a laugh, please! "Well," she said, walking closer while cinching the towel around her waist, "I have anal cancer, and I decided early on that I had to have a sense of humor or I couldn't get through this." From the day of her diagnosis, she said, she'd been writing raunchy poetry about her issue ("and I'm not usually a potty-mouth"), and she and her oncologist had a raucous time making butt jokes, she said. "Every time he says 'but,' I ask, 'Does that have one 't' or two?'" She had just received in the mail from a friend the perfect visual aid for her disease, she announced. She turned around with her back to us and with a little dramatic flair, dropped the towel. There it was, the strange object I'd seen in the car parked next to mine: an enormous, flesh-colored, molded-plastic butt, covering her own (clothed) behind. The room erupted in laughter. After it subsided, I made her promise she would email her butt poetry to me and gave her my email address. But I suspect she later felt a little chagrined by her performance, since I've yet to receive anything. We did have a few moments of serious talk about her condition: Her radiation oncologist has warned her that "you won't like me much" as her radiation burn will cover the entire front and back of her lower abdomen and pelvic area, and her skin will all slough off, she said. I cannot imagine the fear she must have about that, on top of the fear about her disease in general, and the indignity of its location. They called her name before mine, and she trotted off down the hallway, towel once again cinched around her waist. A few seconds later, we heard the radiation therapists burst into laughter when she dropped it.

Human beings have an endless capacity to use humor to retain our sanity. Soldiers in combat, police officers and pathologists all use "gallows humor" to maintain a modicum of equilibrium. I will never forget the woman with the towel. What an exemplar of true character she was. In the face of such courage, I cannot sit on my pity pot for long.

May you find the equivalent of a molded-plastic flesh-colored butt to make you and yours laugh about your troubles this week!

Love,
Hollis

Cancer Journal

April 4

These are notes for the in-service I would like to give at the cancer center, the things I wish caregivers would do in the course of their work with me (and all patients, if I can be so bold as to assume most patients share similar feelings):

(1) Acknowledge my pain. Be truthful about it in advance and acknowledge it when it occurs. Ask me to describe it. Doing so releases some of the anxiety about the pain. When another person truly sees my suffering, it diminishes.

(2) Acknowledge my fear. No one ever asked me if I was afraid of the treatments, or if I was afraid I would be disfigured, or if I was afraid I would never have feeling in my breast like I used to. Ask me what I am afraid of.

(3) Talk to me, not the computer. I know you are busy and I know the computer helps us, but when you look at the screen and chirp, standing eight feet away from me, "Having any pain today?" do you really think I'm going to let you see my pain or suffering? When you ignore me—the human patient—you condemn me to go home with this festering wound to my spirit that is ultimately much worse than my radiated skin, my bald head, my colostomy bag, my limp—whatever my particular physical problems are. "Having any pain today?" shouldn't be a rote question asked only because your computer form demands an answer.

(4) You're thinking, I don't have the time. Yes, you do. Demand the time. It is immoral and unethical not to treat the whole person with respect. Maybe you're also thinking, I can't let in any more suffering than I already feel for my patients. You must. Healing is a two-way event in which the healer also benefits. It's not your fault that you weren't taught how to cope with others' suffering on an emotional/spiritual level, but you can learn.

(5) Listen and observe. You have been trained in clinical assessment. Apply those skills to my emotional and spiritual being. Look at my posture, my eyes, my hands. Am I tense? Dejected? Do I look different, sound different, than I have at previous appointments? Ask, "Are you feeling a little down today?" You can poke and prod me, stick needles in me, radiate and chemo me like mad and I will comply and not complain if I feel the teeniest bit reassured that you care about me as a human being. Find something we have in common to talk about, if only the weather or the upcoming holiday or a new movie.

(6) Touch me. I don't mean in a contrived way. But sit close to me—two feet away at the most. When you take my blood pressure or conduct other exams that require clinical touch, don't do it quickly or with force. Do it a little slower, gently; let your hand pause on my arm. We are both humans; it is only fate, chance, a random act of God, that I am the patient and you are the clinician. Tomorrow you may be in my seat. How would you want to be treated?

Booby Blog #19

April 8

Dear Ones:

I am on the home stretch, with just three more radiation treatments to go as I write this! The last one will be this Thursday, April 11, unless the machine breaks down between now and then, or a major snowstorm prevents me from getting to the cancer center, or something else equally unlikely occurs.

My last six treatments are the "booster" treatments. While the first 28 radiated my entire breast, these focus just on the place where the tumor was. They attach a square device to The Beamer that narrows the beam to a much smaller area and situate the head of The Beamer to my far left. The kind of radiation is different as well: The earlier treatments were photon radiation—"Photons are particles that have no matter, and the beam goes all the way through you," Dr. Gold explained—while the current treatments are electron beams, "which stop when they reach their destination." It doesn't feel any different, and, thankfully, the area of skin affected is much smaller, since I now have a lovely radiation burn that makes my left breast look like it belongs to some exotic island resident, sort of a rich reddish-brown. It doesn't feel too exotic, and lately I've had some additional pain inside my breast ("Well, if your skin is getting burned, imagine what it's doing inside," the doc said). But, overall, I am tolerating the treatments well. And I have made my peace with being the Queen of Naps, giving in to the nonnegotiable fatigue for about an hour's sleep each afternoon.

I have a little trepidation about the post-treatment recovery period. Friends who've been down this path before me say it's not a good idea to expect to return to feeling physically normal right away. One friend said it took a few months before she really felt like herself again. Another said she experienced a curious letdown, a depression, when her treatments were over. "As long as I was going to treatment, I felt like I was doing something active about the cancer," she said. Afterward, she felt rather helpless.

One of the most interesting things I've realized during the radiation treatment is that, during this time, I have had the most consistent spiritual practice of my lifetime. Every single weekday at exactly the same time and for exactly the same *length* of time I lay on that uncomfortable table and prayed while The Beamer "enlightened" me. I started out praying that all the cells that were no longer useful would be released, the healthy cells rejuvenated and new healthy cells inspired to grow. Eventually I just prayed to be able to let go of everything in my life that no longer serves me: resentments, fears, unfounded rage, procrastination, fears, impatience, stored grief, judgment—wait, did I mention fears? And I prayed to expand upon the healthy habits I do have and to acquire some new ones. Those prayers centered me, reminded me of what is really important in my life and made that time sacred. What a gift.

So when Thursday comes, I will be really glad to say goodbye to The Beamer, but I think I'm going to have to figure out a way to keep up the new spiritual practice. It's certainly a good way to start the day. (And this news *just* in—from a "reverend!")

Thanks for listening.

Borrowing from my friend Roy's recent email sign-off, I am Up to my Neck in the Cosmic Overwhelm,

Hollis

Cancer Journal

April 10

Tomorrow will be my last day of radiation. I will miss it in some ways. It had brought structure to my days during a time that has been emotionally chaotic. I am a person who is comforted by routine, as I believe most of us are — at least those of us who as infants and children were contained by a routine of regular meals, naps, playtimes, rules and limitations that parents often impose on their children. Routine — even the routine of The Beamer — has afforded me the illusion that I have been taking a curative action against the cancer and the possibility of its recurrence. In my head I know there are no guarantees, as I have said many times. God "sends rain on the just and the unjust alike (Matthew 5:45)." The only "solution" to this existential angst — because that's truly what it is, at its base — is to live life to its very fullest, every day, and to accept that angst as the legacy of human consciousness.

Booby Blog #20

April 18

Dear Ones:

Last Thursday was my final radiation treatment. Hurrah! It felt somewhat monumental, as you might expect. I said my goodbyes to the radiation therapists and to the man who had shared the waiting room with me every morning for the last several weeks, his appointment following mine. I said a silent goodbye to The Beamer, too. I had a brief check-in with Dr. Gold, whom I hope not to see again (except maybe in the grocery store; this is a small town, after all).

Back in the dressing room, I engaged in a small "reverse" ritual. The blue gown I had refused to wear after my first day of radiation lay in a rumpled pile on a bookshelf in my office at the house throughout my treatment period. I entertained notions of ripping the fabric to shreds and making some sort of cathartic art object with it. But on Thursday, I instead took that ugly blue gown back to the center and in my own secret ceremony, deposited it in the laundry bin in the dressing room, thus shedding my identity as "patient."

When I got home, I took off my clothes and, using some vitamin E oil, carefully peeled off all the surgical tape pieces that had been placed atop the black Sharpie marks on my chest to guide the radiation therapists as they focused The Beamer on me. (I'd been thus taped up throughout the 6 1/2 weeks of daily treatments.) Since my breast skin is very burned from the radiation, it was rather painful, but I managed not to remove any skin in the process—which the therapists had warned me was a very real possibility. Probably *because* it was painful, it, too, had the feeling of an initiation. And voila! Though still reddish-brown, my boob looked like *me* again, without those black targets and tape.

I was thrilled to be done with radiation, but I learned from the nurse that the radiation burn likely will continue to *worsen* for a few weeks before it gets better and that the fatigue that forces me into bed for a nap most afternoons will hang on for a while, too. But these are manageable issues. And now, instead of jumping in the car at 7:30 a.m. and driving to the cancer center, I am instead going to a nearby park along the river trail, where I am once again walking. I've had to accept that it still will be a while before I can run again; the boob bouncing is still too painful, and wearing two jog bras at once is just as uncomfortable due to the smashing factor! (I did try holding my left boob firmly with my left hand while running, but it cramped my jogging style, and I couldn't help but feel a wee bit self-conscious as I passed others on the trail.)

My last appointment for some time with my oncologist was great. We rehashed the statistics about recurrence (I have an 80 percent chance of being breast cancer-free over the next 10 years, or, put the opposite way, a 20 percent chance of recurrence, he said) and the protocol for follow-up: mammograms every six months on the affected breast for a year and every year on the other breast for the foreseeable future. Once I pass the year mark, I'll just have annual mammograms on both boobs. When he walked into the exam room where I was waiting, I was in the midst of reading an article critiquing the efficacy of mammograms. It noted how researchers who have raised questions about this sacred cow are vilified in their professions and in the medical world in general. My doc offered that the use of mammography in general remains controversial. Imagine! A physician who admits that the medical institution *just might be wrong*. Didn't I luck out the second time around when I got this doctor? We also revisited my decision not to take aromatase inhibitors, the drugs that block estrogen and thus are believed to decrease even further the chance of breast cancer recurrence. The doctor affirmed my rationale—without recommending either route—and we made a date in August to see each other again once I've had my first follow-up mammogram.

On Friday I engaged in another end-of-radiation ritual: I sat down and wrote thank-you notes to each of the people who had cared for me during radiation, including four radiation therapists, three nurses, the radiation oncologist and the most important person in the center: the receptionist who had greeted me by name and with a smile the first time and every time I came through the cancer center door. Hers was the longest note of all.

When I dropped the notes off and was about to leave, I ran into the woman I wrote about a few weeks ago who has anal cancer and had worn a molded-plastic butt to her treatment just for laughs. She'd told me she wrote raunchy poems about her cancer, and I had given her my email and asked her to send me some. We greeted each other like friends, and I admonished her, "Hey, I thought you were going to send me poems!" Right there in the parking lot she pulled one up on her phone and I laughed my—er—butt off. I'm sure we were a curious sight, giggling together, since there isn't much laughter going on at the cancer center. Since then, she's sent me several of the poems. Most of them are limericks you just wouldn't believe. Unfortunately, she asked me not to share them in writing, but suffice it to say that she affirmed my heartfelt belief that creativity—and especially humor—is the surest path through suffering.

As I write this today, I am sitting in Taos at a friend's casita, so generously loaned to me again for a little writing retreat. I have returned to the memoir I started several years ago with renewed motivation. Our time here on Earth is limited, and we usually are not privy to knowing exactly *how* limited. Cancer has made that clearer to me than ever before. So, I'm asking you today, in the words of the poet Mary Oliver, "Tell me, what is it you plan to do/ with your one wild and precious life?"

Thank you for listening and for your unwavering support, my dear friends!

Love,
Hollis

Cancer Journal

April 20

I wrote my 20th Booby Blog the other day, about my last radiation treatment, and was very interested when I received emails back from several people congratulating me not just on completing radiation but also on completing the blog!

I realize that response was perfectly rational. I'd finished my treatment and could now proceed with my life, putting this all behind me and hoping for the best, right?

But I know for me that is not true. I must resist the idea of returning to life as usual, life as before breast cancer, or I will lose the great lessons it has offered me. I do want to move forward, and I certainly do not want to remain mired in obsessive thinking about illness and death or to be forever afraid that every new freckle is a sign the cancer has returned. But I am not done learning from this and sense there may be a bit more I can share as I go along. So maybe I will write a few more entries before I stop and then (hopefully) add an epilogue post in August, when I get my clear mammogram.

I feel a bit like I am standing in the bottom of an old, dried-up well, looking up from the dark, past the worn walls to the light above. My hands are cupped around my mouth and I am calling, "Yoo-hoo! Anyone up there?" I need an assist, someone to lower the bucket rope, so I can somehow fasten it around myself and be cranked up to the light, to rejoin the real world. I want to see a vast horizon, green grass and big trees. I am not entirely certain I'm ready for a homecoming party, though. Rather, I feel I can handle only a few people at a time as I readjust to this, my brave new world. Maybe this cancer has been the epilogue to my years of self-examination and discovery, which started in April 2008. Here it is five years later. Time to re-emerge from the dark womb?

Booby Blog #21

May 13

Dear Ones,

So you're thinking, what's this? Another Booby Blog? Didn't she say she was *done* with her treatments?

Well, yes, but I am finding true what my friends who've been down this path before told me: It's not over just because the treatment had ended. Treatment offers an agenda; it drives one's days, structures and distracts and keeps one focused. Without it, I feel a bit purposeless on one hand, while on another I yearn to have my full energy back *now* for an "assault" on the future.

Instead, most days I feel like a bear wandering out of hibernation, slow and lumbering, yawning and scratching, squinting into the sun, wondering idly where I might get a good meal. A little tempted to crawl back into my cave. Definitely still in need of a daily nap.

And speaking of which, what should I do about the self-care protocol my "alternative" M.D. prescribed—the 20 supplements a day, the acupuncture, the infrared sauna, etc. Keep it up? Relax it a bit? Or would that tempt fate? The big Mexican dinner I cheated on the other night (a friend's birthday party) didn't just tempt Fate. "Fate"(a.k.a. my gastrointestinal system) got pissed off big time! I was sick as a dog for 24 hours, not being used to the rich and spicy fare. (Be very glad you weren't in my household during that day and night!) Back to plain chicken and rice.

Despite all this, I do have good news. I am back to walking daily, though still not up to running. The "bounce" factor is still too unpleasant. The other day, I was digging through bras in my intimates drawer, trying to find the tightest one, and I discovered the gigantic, ugly, stretchy, white nylon thing they gave me to wear post-surgery. I had an impromptu ritual and deposited it in the trash can; its usefulness in my life is *over*! More happy bra news: The other day I was able to wear without serious discomfort one of my "pretty" bras from the pre-cancer days. Woohoo! My breast still hurts, but these days it's a different kind of pain, which I assume must be a sign of healing. Bring it on!

But most importantly, the other day I had coffee with a friend who was diagnosed with breast cancer about the same time I was. She is in her 30s, married, the mother of an amazing little 7-year-old girl who reminds me of myself as a child: dark-haired, skinny, a mischievous spirit. My friend had a double mastectomy and now is facing her second round of chemotherapy, to be followed by radiation. We talked about our experiences in between her gentle admonishments to her daughter (who was reluctantly working on her homework), and I was absolutely humbled and amazed. How is it that this woman, facing life-threatening illness and such terrible personal suffering, can still be so patient, be such a wonderful mommy? I wish I could re-create for you the conversation I heard her have with her little one off and on during our chat. What a gift and inspiration to witness my friend's love and support for her child. I am sure Mother's Day this year has an even deeper meaning for her than usual. May we all be so devoted to someone in our lives that we can put aside our own suffering in service to that beloved one!

Whew. Sometimes I have "big" days when I least expect them.

So, my friends, I expect there will be a few more of these missives before I call the "Booby Blog" done. Thanks for your indulgence and your calls and emails to check in since I completed treatment!

Love,
Hollis

Booby Blog #22

October 1

I feel I need to write this final Booby Blog to close this chapter of my life, at least symbolically. It has been almost a year ago now since the day I woke up and heard The Voice saying, "You have a lump in your left breast." A few weeks ago I saw my oncologist, having had my first follow-up mammogram, and he gave me the "all-clear," at least for the time being. He now says I have a 90 percent chance of remaining cancer free.

So much has happened during the last year that it's hard for me to comprehend, even now. I am sure anyone who has cancer or another medical crisis feels much the same way. Whiplashed. Flattened on the road like the old cartoon character Wile E. Coyote. Confused, like the Scarecrow when Dorothy first discovers him in *The Wizard of Oz*—tied to his post and pointing in *both* directions. *Now* what?

I had a few friends who expressed surprise that I wasn't back in the saddle as soon as treatments were over. In fact, I developed greater fatigue and really horrid gastrointestinal problems (I'll spare you details) that persisted for months after the radiation ended. Have you ever piled so much stuff on a closet shelf that one day the pile reaches critical mass? You toss a sweater up there, and the whole stack comes tumbling down in your face? That's sort of what happened with the emotional backwash, once I got through all the treatments and the gut troubles subsided. I had to start tangling with my feelings. Thankfully, my friends who have been through this before me reassured me that it was all perfectly ordinary. Without those friends I would have been in bad shape, since not one single medical caregiver ever mentioned the emotional aspects of this illness. Hard to believe, isn't it?

In the months since I finished treatment, my work as a chaplain and minister has begun to develop again, for which I'm grateful.

During my illness, one of my friends who was on this Bosom Buddies list was diagnosed with lung cancer and died. I was able to sit with her as a chaplain during her last weeks of life. Another dear friend fell suddenly ill at the end of July, and I had the privilege of being with him and his wife during the last month of his life — and of officiating at his memorial. Three of my friends in California were diagnosed with breast cancer, and I was able on a recent trip to see two of them and offer my experience and hope. The women's support group I facilitate has continued throughout my treatment—and helped keep me sane!—and my private spiritual and writing coaching clientele is slowly growing.

My life is reorganizing itself, and I continue to recover.

If there is anything I have learned from this experience, it is that we need to say the important things *now*. What are those? Please forgive me for any harm I may have done you, intentional or not. I forgive you for any harm you may have done me. Thank you for all that you have contributed to my life. And—most important of all—I love you! [13]

Thank you for sharing this journey with me.

Love,
Hollis

---

13 The paragraph about the important things we need to say was inspired by Ira Bayock, M.D.'s book, *The Four Things That Matter Most: A Book About Living.*

Epilogue

February 26

Many years ago, I had to drive from Santa Fe to Farmington, New Mexico, and decided that I would take scenic State Road 4, which winds off into the wilderness near the town of Los Alamos, through the Santa Fe National Forest. Something curious happened along the way, and I got lost. I found myself bouncing and bumping along a muddy track, having never made a turn that I could recall. The road—if you could call it that—was wet with the spring snowmelt and full of huge holes and ruts. The shade of the tall, stately pines, which had seemed so beautiful a short time before, now seemed menacing; I could barely glimpse the sky above them. My trusty old all-wheel-drive Subaru strained mightily to ascend the hills I encountered, and the road demanded first gear most of the time. Where was I? How had I gotten here? I couldn't turn around; there wasn't room—no shoulders on this not-a-road. I was lost in a "dark wood," to borrow Dante's language.

So it was with my cancer. I had a plan for my life, and cancer interrupted it, in a shocking and terrifying way. But not everything about the experience was bad. In fact, you might say it was necessary to my growth. As Dante explains in the familiar introduction to Canto I of *The Inferno*,

> *In the middle of the journey of our life, I came to myself, in a dark wood,*
> *where the direct way was lost. It is a hard thing to speak of, how wild, harsh*
> *and impenetrable that wood was, so that thinking of it recreates the fear.*
> *It is scarcely less bitter than death: but, in order to tell of the good that I*
> *found there, I must tell of the other things I saw there.*

It is now more than a year since I found the lump in my breast, more than a year since I had my lumpectomy. When my radiation treatment ended, and again later, when I got the "all clear" after my first post-treatment mammogram, I felt I should be further along than I was. Shouldn't I be back at work full time, back on the treadmill, trying to make up for the time lost to cancer? Shouldn't I be really happy, even downright cheerful, since I had a clean bill of health and a good prognosis?

Instead I felt at odds with myself, as if an internal battle were being waged. The "old me" was arguing for a return to the status quo, to put it all behind me and pretend that was the last time I'd ever hear that dog bark. But the "new me" demurred. Did I really want to turn my back on all I had gained, for which I had paid so dearly?

What had I learned, anyway? Had I just romanticized or idealized my experience as a compensatory mechanism? Yet it seemed to me that I *had* learned a great deal. I had learned a lot about cancer. I had also added to the knowledge base I had developed as a chaplain about today's medical institutions and how they work — or more often, *fail* to work. And I'd been reminded that medical caregivers often are anything but *care* givers and that, for many complicated reasons, the very people who are supposed to be healing the patient have forgotten that the patient is a person.

But mostly, cancer had brought into focus my own beliefs: about illness, mortality, God, personal responsibility, healing and identity.

No medical scientist can lay claim to understanding the cause of illness. No one can say why two people with similar genetic makeup can live side by side in the same environment and share similar lifestyles and one gets cancer and dies at 50 while the other lives hale and hearty until dying in her sleep at 95. Though some religions and primitive peoples once interpreted illness as a sign of God's wrath, and others believe God "gives us" illnesses so that we can learn from them, most people recognize on some level that a hallmark of illness is its randomness. Yet our culture also teaches us, overtly and covertly, that we are to blame for much of our illness. When we hear that someone we know has lung cancer, the first thing we ask is, "Did he smoke?" Because if he smoked, we can blame it on the smoking — on his choice to smoke — and therefore reassure ourselves that it won't happen to us, because we don't smoke. We use causality as a meme to protect ourselves from the chaos and fear that arise when we accept that *it can and may in fact happen to us, no matter what we do.* "It" being illness, in the short term, and death, in the final analysis.

During my illness, I recognized that as much as I am skeptical of the medical and healing communities (allopathic, Eastern, alternative, all of them), I still harbored an unconscious belief in the physician as representative of an ultimate authority. I wanted to believe that somewhere out there was a cache of truths that would lead to my healing. Intellectually, I knew that nothing about illness or healing is certain or absolute, and no one has all the answers. But in my heart, I wanted to believe in that ultimate authority, and on some days I had to, just to get through whatever challenge was facing me in the moment.

Of course I knew I was mortal. Hadn't I sat at the bedsides of many dying people? Hadn't I watched some of them take their last breaths? Didn't I see and accept that this body is a biological system that eventually, like all other such systems, breaks down and ceases to function? Yes, but my cancer was the first concrete evidence that *mine* was going to do so, and the suggestion that it might do so long before the requisite "she's lived a good, long life" could be uttered. I might not make it to my mother's age of 85. But I also saw that illness is part of life, that those who are ill should not be made to be Other. We should talk about our illnesses, say out loud, "I have cancer," or, "I'm dealing with diabetes," not be afraid to acknowledge that illness is part of the path we are all on — to destigmatize, to normalize, illness.

Though my concept of God had already evolved considerably, especially in seminary, some small part of me persisted in believing in what a friend calls "the Santy Claus God," a transcendent being who is going to grant my every wish, fill my stocking, cure me if I am good enough. I had to continue giving up that God, day by day, and embracing the God that I could honestly accept: a transcendent and immanent presence that is without form, without name, beyond gender and beyond human explanation. This is the God who whispered to me in my half-wake state that I had a lump in my breast. This is the God who prompted me to wear my leopard-spotted robe and reject a passive, compliant identity as "patient." This is the God who urged me out on my first post-treatment run (despite my full-on face plant, or maybe because of it). As a minister and spiritual director, I had many times suggested that those whose God was negative, harsh or unloving "get a new God." During my illness, I took my own best advice.

I thought I had always been very responsible for myself, earning a living, participating in my community, trying to be "a good person." Often that meant focusing on others and their needs, which was the purpose for which I was raised as a female born into a middle-class Christian home in 1960s and '70s America. What I gained while I had cancer was the fierce and protective love of a mother for a child—with *me* in both roles. I had to put everyone else aside, let go of any hubris that I could "help" anyone else, and help myself. Somehow I also came to understand that this shift was not a temporary program of self-love to get me through the cancer but should become a permanent mind-set. Help myself, take care of myself and my needs, and then and only then, if there are remaining resources, offer them to others. I am not capable of helping others if my own house is not in order. And—though it seems somehow contradictory, in the larger philosophical sense—I had to let others help me. I had to be dependent, as if I were a child again. I had to shut up, accept help, say thank you.

In a way, having cancer afforded me the opportunity to revisit and heal the suffering of my childhood. The chronic illness I had as a child wasn't the worst of it. I suffered because of the complete loss of control I felt, the dehumanizing aspects of illness and abuse by medical personnel. Those childhood experiences and my work as a hospital and hospice chaplain had prepared me well for what I faced. I determined I would take better care of myself as an adult than I was able to as a child. For the most part, I was able to do so. I stood up for myself when I felt I was being disregarded or mistreated, ignored or dismissed. I refused to embody the "good patient" and instead focused on making the best decisions for me. I accepted responsibility for learning all I could and making those decisions, regardless of outcomes. I came away from that experience more convinced than ever that I wanted to help other women see that they can and must empower themselves to recover fully. Recovery from an illness takes many forms, not the least of which is psycho-spiritual.

One of the most shocking discoveries I made about the extreme vulnerability of being sick was that the vulnerability that was most painful wasn't feeling exposed physically or emotionally to other people (although that was indeed painful) but that illness stripped me down to my core, and I saw *myself* more clearly than ever before. I saw my attributes and my failings, my foolhardy way of walking through life, what I had lost or missed and could never regain. I saw myself naked, as if seen by God, and I was humbled. One of the lovely side effects of that gut-wrenching experience is that I am no longer quite so afraid to allow others to see me. I can now choose to be more honest, vulnerable and emotionally bare with others. Oddly, this feels really good. Nothing is held back. I am not lying, literally or figuratively, anymore. I am somewhat more assured that the way out of the dark wood will always appear if I have faith and just keep driving.

On that muddy, rutted road I found myself on in the forest that day long ago, I just kept driving, because I had no choice. Eventually the pines parted, the sky reappeared, and a road—a real road, with asphalt!—presented itself. Just as I had accidentally left the pavement, I had accidentally rediscovered it. I had somehow gotten back to State Road 4. My mud-covered car happily dragged itself out of the muck and onto the smooth, safe surface, and as I looked in the rear-view mirror, I noticed a wide metal gate propped open against a tree, and from it hung a sign that read, "Forest Service Road, Do Not Enter." I still don't know how I got on that road, nor how I found my way out. But I certainly will never forget the trip.

Acknowledgements

Many people eased my journey with cancer. I am grateful to Karen Zeligson, Mollie Busbey, Rev. Pandora Canton, Victoria Price and Cynthia Lucius. Monika Wikman and members of the Isis Group were essential to my sanity. I deeply appreciate the use of my friend Alexandra Eldridge's beautiful art for the book's cover and the photograph of me by Kitty Leaken.

Despite my criticisms and distrust of our medical system, many of the people I encountered were respectful and compassionate. I am grateful to all of them.

My thanks to readers of *The Booby Blog: A Cancer Chronicle* as it was in progress: Andy Dudzik, Larry Dossey, M.D., Rev. Shelby Morales, R.N., Sally Ooms, Amy Sayers and Joni Tickel.

Most of all, I am grateful to the readers of the original Booby Blog, whose affirmation helped me believe in myself and my future.

Finally, my humble thanks to these special friends of The Booby Blog Project: Marisa Again, Michael Allison, M.D., Susan Amick, Kurt Anderson, Anne Fay, Lolly Bair, Joan Brooks Baker, Carolyn Clark Beedle, Vanessa Benavides, Gina Browning, Nancy Clark and Jody Dufresne, Lee Cobb and Lucilo Pena, Cornbread, Mary Curry and Kelly Hyde, Jeff Fenton and Christopher Martinez, Carroll Geddie, Renata Golden, Lynn Marchand Goldstein, Roberta Golub, Kim and Rose Griego-Kiel, Victoria Hall, Anne Hillerman, Tanya Gazdik Irwin, Margeaux Klein, Jeanine Koehler, Sue LeGrand, Catherine Owens, Park, Nancy Pearce, Maria Poulides and Nan Palmer, Ph.D., Debbie Ramirez, Gail Richards, Christopher Rocca and David Rosen, Jay Rosenbaum, Cathi Scalise, Lauren Scott, Rev. Michael Stamper, Cyndy and Steve Tanner, Evelyn Walker, Melissa Weiner, George and Ruth Weston, Danny and Debbie Zeligson, and Nelson and Chelona Zink.

CPSIA information can be obtained at www.ICGtesting.com
Printed in the USA
LVOW05s0633201014

409426LV00004B/7/P

9 780990 570707